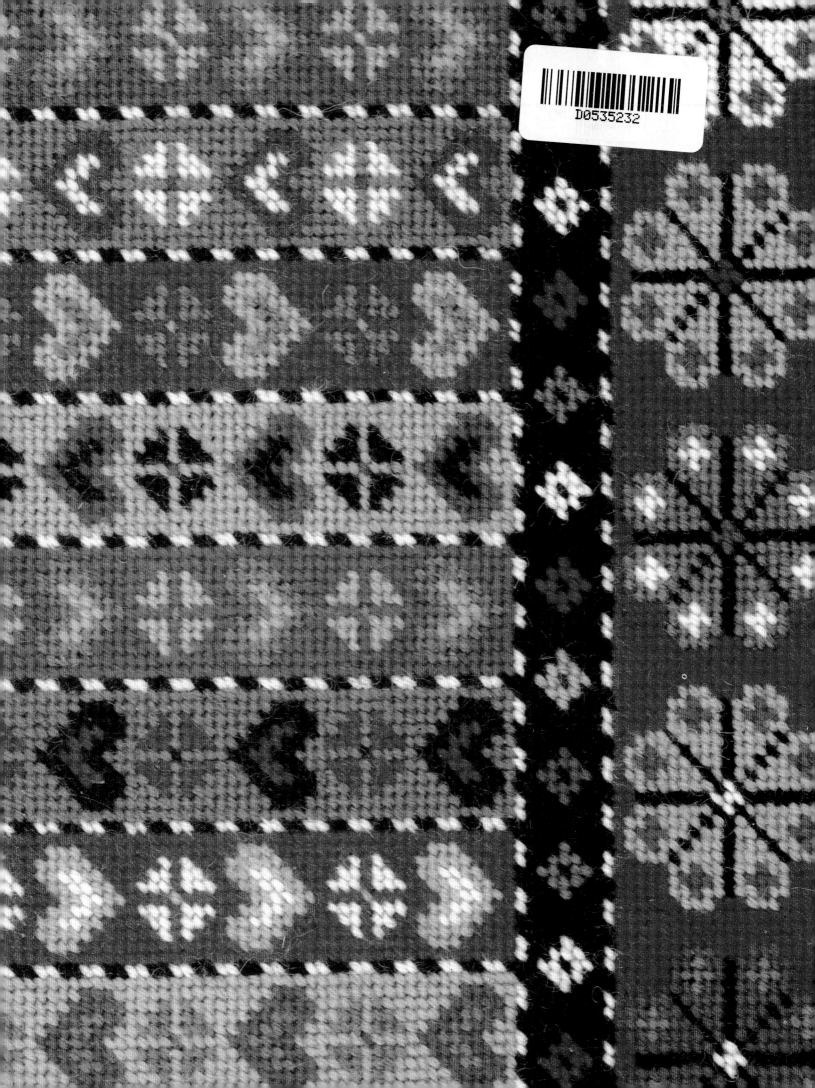

Mary Norden's Needlepoint

MARY NORDEN'S
Needlepoint

fifty

folk art

projects for

the home

PHOTOGRAPHS BY NADIA MACKENZIE

Weidenfeld and Nicolson

LONDON

First published in 1994 by
George Weidenfeld &
Nicolson Ltd
Orion House
5 Upper St Martin's Lane
London WC2H 9EA

British Library
Cataloguing-in-
Publication Data
A catalogue record for this
book is available from the
British Library.

ISBN 0 297 83265 4

Designed by Roger Davies
Charts by Malcolm Couch
Illustrations by
Sarah Davies
Styled by Mary Norden
Jacket design by the Senate
Colour separations by
Newsele Litho Ltd
Printed in Italy by
Printers Srl, Trento
Bound by L.E.G.O.,
Vicenza

Contents

Introduction

11

Introduction

A question I am frequently asked as a designer is, 'Where do you find the inspiration for your work?' and I always tell people just to continually look. Colour and pattern can be found in everything.

My first (and still one of the best) sources of inspiration were illustrated books and magazines. As a child I spent hours poring over them, devouring them as though they were chocolates and often extending my obsession late into the night with the aid of a torch and makeshift tent made out of my blankets. It didn't matter that I couldn't read them, I was only interested in the imagery and the glossy colours: foreign cities with magnificent buildings sometimes adorned with mosaic patterns, exotic birds and fish striped with jewel-like colours, and dancing tribes with bodies painted in wild abstract patterns. In addition to looking at pictures I avidly collected them: postcards, magazine and newspaper cuttings, cigarette and tea cards. I could have won prizes for my scrapbooks, so stuffed were they with colourful pictures. Thus began an abiding fascination with colour and pattern.

At art college I studied textile design and it was here that new and exciting possibilities were opened up to me. To this day I derive inspiration from continually visiting museums and exhibitions, walking through gardens at the height of summer, watching films, rushing to markets at six in the morning, gazing at window displays, particularly those dressed for Christmas, and wandering through food halls looking not just at the food but at the packaging. I am like a squirrel always searching and hoarding ideas and colour combinations to stimulate new designs.

From this hoard I chose the world of folk art for my inspiration for this, my second book on needlepoint design. It is a fascinating world that I continually return to for inspiration, so

rich and diverse in pattern and colour, all as a result of man's constant urge to decorate and adorn not just his home but also his furniture, textiles and utensils. The majority of the people who created these objects, sought their living from the soil. They had no formal art training and did not make a distinction between works of art and objects for use

It is a world that has now largely disappeared. By the end of the nineteenth century and the beginning of the twentieth, cities were developing, factories were being built, bridges were crossing rivers and a network of railways was weaving it's way across countries linking different regions. With this there developed an industrial society of mass production which inevitably led to great changes. Traditional skills were abandoned, for example a woman would no longer spend several months or even years on a costume made of materials that she herself had spun and woven.

But today in our consumer world, where technology threatens to take over completely and is capable of creating soulless perfection, we look nostalgically to a more simple, rustic lifestyle. There is an enormous resurgence of interest in not only this earthier way of life but also in the naive charm of folk artefacts, each with its own individuality. Anyone visiting a museum of folk art or looking at books on this art form from the various regions of Europe and America cannot but be delighted and bewildered by the wealth of imagination and ingenuity found in the decorative traditions. Everywhere glossy home interest magazines, shops, interiors, advertisements, even restaurants strive to convey this uncluttered style: fabrics in traditional patterns and colours woven in natural fibres and furniture and utensils in simple timeless shapes are once again extraordinarily popular. Original pieces of folk art are now avidly sought after by museums and collectors worldwide and people have at last

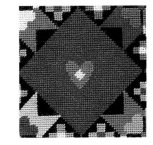

become aware of the visual language and the enormous richness of this art form.

In response to folk art establishing itself as the look and lifestyle of the nineties and with the lack of designs encapsulating the many colourful features of folk art ornamentation, I decided to create my own collection of needlepoint designs. I explored the peasant cultures of Scandinavia, Europe - particularly Eastern Europe - and the early settlers of America during the eighteenth and nineteenth centuries. However, the range is so vast and diverse that I had to limit myself to something more manageable, so I decided to focus on the domestic culture of these people. As a textile designer I was initially drawn specifically to the home textiles, whether it be the complex floral rugs of Romania or the red and white embroidery that adorns a Hungarian pillowcase, but once I had began my research, I was equally captivated and inspired by the furniture, kitchen utensils, tools, dishes and the wall decorations and became overwhelmed with ideas.

The range of objects included in this book, from the smallest of bags to the directors chair will I hope offer something for everyone and will illustrate that there are so many different ways needlepoint can be used. Cushions are always fun and challenging to stitch but there is a limit to how many you can have on your sofa. The smaller pieces make ideal gifts that would give lasting pleasure. At the other end of the scale many of the patterns, particularly the repeat patterns, can be extended to cover a piece of furniture of any shape or size.

I hope when you read this book and are stitching some of the designs that you will feel the same excitement that I felt whilst creating this collection. It should encourage less experienced needlepointers and will stimulate a creative interest in everyone so that you will feel confident and inspired to progress to designing your own patterns.

CHAPTER ONE

Hearts
and
Garlands

When I look at folk art, whether it be the colourful rose paintings of Norway, the appliquéd quilts of Baltimore or the flamboyant embroideries of Hungary, I am drawn into a world of endless imaginary gardens, each one filled to bursting point with flowers and foliage. Throughout folk culture floral patterns were lavished onto walls, furniture, utensils and most frequently of all onto textiles, each object expressing the peasants' love of flowers: tulips, carnations and roses were arranged with native species from the peasants' own garden such as hyacinths, peonies and geraniums. The most popular of these stylized arrangements was the 'flowers in the pot' motif and the garland of flowers and leaves. The 'flower in the pot' design combined a two handled vase with one or more richly flowered stems and was frequently used as a single motif to fill a whole surface, for example a cushion. It represented the tree of life, unless the vase was replaced by a heart, as was common in the embroidery of a brides' dowry, and then its meaning became one of love. The garland in its most basic form was a wavy line with leaves and flowers sprouting out in all directions. Single garlands were rare. Both hearts and garlands were a favourite motif in textile design: woven along borders of pillow cases, embroidered onto headdresses, skirts and bodices, cross-stitched into samplers and appliquéd onto quilts.

Floral patterns appeared on furniture and utensils, from the rims of painted plates where garlands framed a central motif to the large acanthus leaf carvings of northern Europe which

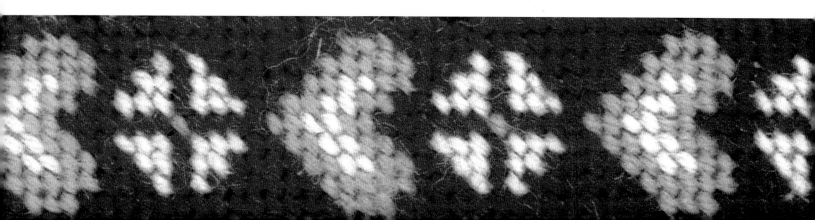

covered drinking vessels as well as clothes chests. Traditionally however, the heart was often the most important motif, being used to decorate utensils, in particular objects which were associated with women's household tasks, such as laundry beaters, mangling boards, weaving implements and yokes for carrying water buckets. These utensils were usually lover's gifts which were presented on the occasion of an engagement as proof of a man's promise to marry. At weddings the heart was used extensively, not just on presents but also on the plates, bowls and jugs used for the celebrations. Its shape was made up of garlands of flowers and leaves, frequently for the purpose of framing the names of the bridal couple, the date and maybe a motto relating to love and marriage.

The heart was also frequently used on furniture in the brides' dowry to bring good fortune to a marriage and to ward away evil and was usually incorporated into an overall pattern with other motifs. For example the doors of Swedish dressers were often painted with hearts and floral designs, in Austria decorative spoon shelves had hearts in carved openwork and in Germany the backs of wooden bridal chairs were decorated with hearts and compass-drawn motifs. On wrought-iron objects used at the hearth, the heart motif was simply used in a decorative way with no symbolic meaning. Even kitchen utensils: baking trays, waffle irons, ramekins, cheese and butter moulds could not escape the heart motif, so any one of my designs which follow will make a perfect token of love, affection and goodwill.

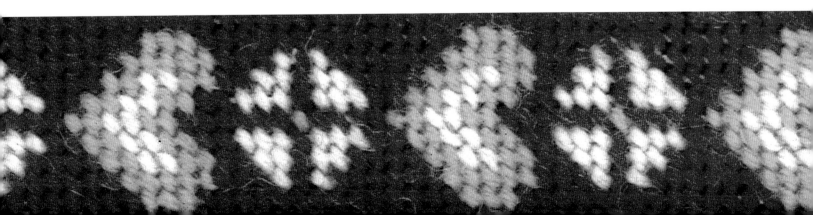

LADY'S BOUQUET

My Lady's Bouquet cushion was directly inspired by the exquisitely stitched quilts of nineteenth-century America, or as I call them, America's Labours of Love, and in particular the album quilts. These were constructed of many separate pictorial blocks, usually appliquéd, and made by a group of women. Each woman contributing blocks to the quilt would design and stitch these at home before they were joined together, usually at a formal album party, into a quilt intended as a gift for a special occasion such as a wedding, a farewell, or even a man's twenty-first birthday (in which case it was known as a freedom quilt!). To create my own

miniature album style needlepoint I designed four blocks each depicting a stylized bouquet of flowers. This is a motif that appears in many quilts in endless variations, sometimes elaborate, sometimes as naive as a child's painting.

To accentuate the album theme and also to hold the composition together I made a feature of the grid between the four blocks by framing each bouquet with a simple row of triangles and diamonds. I then chose an abundance of brilliant colours, first used against a cream background which is very traditional in quilt making and then secondly against a black background for an even richer effect.

LADY'S BOUQUET

Materials

Yarn
DMC tapestry wool in the following colours and approximate amounts.

Cushion

Colourway A
Cream background

Ecru	23	Skeins
7432	1	Skein
7329	2	Skeins
7377	1	Skein
7421	1	Skein
7426	1	Skein
7512	1	Skein
7473	2	Skeins
7304	2	Skeins
7306	1	Skein

LADY'S BOUQUET

7202   2 Skeins

7107   6 Skeins

7241   1 Skein

7724   1 Skein

LADY'S BOUQUET *continued*

Cushion

Colourway B
Black background

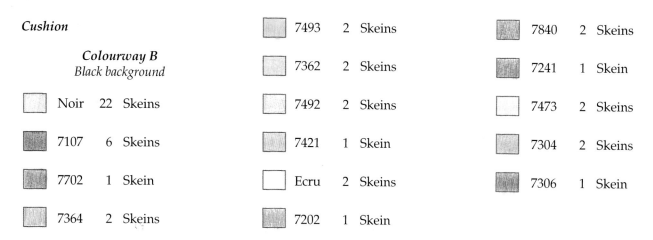

Noir	22	Skeins
7107	6	Skeins
7702	1	Skein
7364	2	Skeins
7493	2	Skeins
7362	2	Skeins
7492	2	Skeins
7421	1	Skein
Ecru	2	Skeins
7202	1	Skein
7840	2	Skeins
7241	1	Skein
7473	2	Skeins
7304	2	Skeins
7306	1	Skein

LADY'S BOUQUET *continued*

Canvas
12-mesh single canvas 21½" (54cm) square.

Finishing Materials
½yd (50cm) of backing fabric and matching thread. 14" (35cm) zip fastener. 71" (180cm) of piping cord or ready made cord for edging (optional). 17" (44cm) square cushion pad.

Charted Design Area
209 stitches wide x 209 stitches high.

Finished Design
17½" (44.5cm) square.

Order Of Work
For full practical information on methods used in 'order of work', refer to Needlepoint Techniques (pages 144-55). Prepare the canvas. The entire design is worked in tent stitch using 1 strand of yarn throughout. Each square on the chart represents one stitch on the canvas. Following the chart, complete the design, working in either colourway A, as given with the chart, or in colourway B by referring to the photograph. Work the background colour last. Stretch the finished needlepoint, before backing. Sew on cord if required.

Each bouquet would work equally well as a framed picture and as the top of a footstool. For something really dramatic, work separate squares of needlepoint and join them together to make a rug. (see Techniques page 153).

BALTIMORE FRUITS

For a seemingly endless source of design material you have to look no further than the American patchwork quilt. The first quilts in the eighteenth century were made by thrifty women for warmth and were an early form of recycling: scraps of fabric were saved from worn out garments and then sewn together into often bold prismatic patterns. In the mid-nineteenth century quilt-making was at its most sophisticated and particularly notable examples came from Baltimore. Using the appliqué technique the local women created brilliantly coloured pictorial quilts that contained not only the traditional motifs of quilt-making, such as vases and wreaths of flowers, wicker baskets, and cornucopias of fruit, but also new and innovative designs inspired by objects of local significance, such as well-known buildings and monuments. Sometimes a woman spent years on a single quilt using fabrics with highly personal associations, such as pieces from Mamma's wedding dress or from curtains she had put up when she was first married.

My Baltimore Fruits cushion with its classic wreath of ribbons and flowers framing a basket of pears, apples, grapes and even a pineapple portrays a little of the richness and complexities of pattern to be found in American quilts.

B A L T I M O R E   F R U I T S

Materials

Yarn
DMC tapestry wool in the following colours and approximate amounts.

Cushion

		Colourway A Cream background	Colourway B Red background
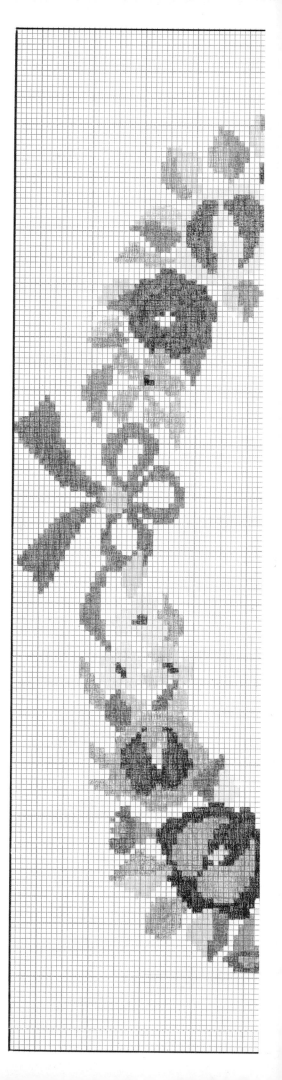	Ecru	15 Skeins	2 Skeins
	7108	3 Skeins	2 Skeins
	7432	2 Skeins	2 Skeins
	7306	2 Skeins	2 Skeins
	7329	2 Skeins	2 Skeins
	7377	1 Skein	1 Skein
	7426	1 Skein	-
	7512	1 Skein	1 Skein
	7202	1 Skein	1 Skein
	7473	2 Skeins	2 Skeins
	7767	2 Skeins	2 Skeins
	7421	1 Skein	1 Skein
	7692	1 Skein	1 Skein
	7927	1 Skein	1 Skein
	7304	1 Skein	1 Skein
	7241	1 Skein	-
	7724	-	1 Skein
	7362	-	1 Skein

Canvas
12-mesh single canvas 20" (50cm) square.

Finishing Materials
½yd (50cm) of backing fabric and matching thread. 14" (35cm) zip fastener. 64" (162cm) of piping cord or ready made cord for edging (optional). 16" (40cm) square cushion pad.

Charted Design Area
187 stitches wide x 194 stitches high.

Finished Design
15½" (39cm) x 16" (40.5cm).

Order Of Work
For full practical information on methods used in 'order of work', refer to Needlepoint Techniques (pages 145–55). Prepare the canvas. The entire design is worked in tent stitch using 1 strand of yarn throughout. Each square on the chart represents one stitch on the canvas. To complete the design in colourway A follow the chart exactly as given. For colourway B, except for a few small changes of colour and the obvious reversal of cream (Ecru) and red (7108) the arrangement of colour remains the same as for colourway A. The few colour changes are as follows: green (7426) is replaced by a slightly paler green (7462); the tiny amounts of purple (7241) are omitted altogether and those areas are stitched in more of the pink (7202); the pieces of fruit worked in red are replaced with a soft beige (7724) rather than cream. When working colourway B, refer not only to the chart but also to the photograph for these colour changes. For both colourways work the background colour last. Stretch the finished needlepoint before backing. Sew on cord if required.

LOVER'S TULIP

In my search through books and museum visits for a heart pattern to translate into needlepoint I came across an exquisite pair of eighteenth-century wool mittens from Sweden, colourfully embroidered in silk and each with a heart surrounded by a spray of stylized carnations, tulips and roses. I learnt that they had belonged to a married women and according to tradition would have been given to her by her husband as an engagement present, thus the use of the heart motif in the embroidery.

I was so charmed by them I wanted to keep my design as close as possible to the original. However, this did not include the choice of colours. The traditional colours for Swedish folk embroidery are bright yellow, green, blue and red on either a cream or black background. Instead I chose fresh blues and greens.

L O V E R ' S   T U L I P

Materials

Yarn
DMC tapestry wool in the following colours and approximate amounts.

Cushion

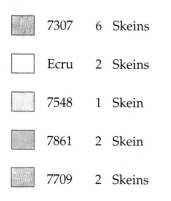

7307	6	Skeins
Ecru	2	Skeins
7548	1	Skein
7861	2	Skein
7709	2	Skeins

Canvas
12-mesh interlock canvas 12" (30cm) x 14" (35cm)

Finishing Materials
A piece of backing fabric 12" (32cm) square. Two pieces of stiff cardboard 9½" (24cm) x 10¼" (26.5cm.) One piece of thinner cardboard or heavy paper for lining 19" (48cm) x 10½ (26.5cm.) Two pieces of ribbon or tape 10" (25cm) long. Masking tape, strong glue.

Charted Design Area
95 stitches wide x 125 stitches high.

Finished Design
8" (20cm) x 10½" (26.5cm).

Completed Folder
9½" (24cm) x 10½" (26.5cm) high.

Order Of Work
For full practical information on methods used in order of work refer to Needlepoint Techniques (pages 144-55). Prepare the canvas. The entire design is worked in half cross stitch using 1 strand of yarn throughout. Each square on the chart represents one stitch on the canvas. Following the chart, complete the design. Stretch the finished needlepoint before making up into a folder. Do not cut excess canvas at this stage. With right sides facing pin and tack backing fabric to needlepoint along left side edge only. Stitch as close to the needlepoint as possible, using a small back stitch or a sewing machine. Trim seam. Press. With masking tape join the two pieces of stiff cardboard along one 10¼" (26cm) side edge, taping on both sides to form a spine. Position cardboard piece open over back of needlepoint and backing fabric

making sure you have a 1½" (4cm) width of fabric along left side edge of needlepoint and to the front of the folder. Trim excess canvas leaving a 1" (2.5cm) overlap all round. The height of the cardboard should be slightly shorter than the height of the needlepoint so as to allow the outer row of stitches to overlap the card on the inside. If this is not possible, trim the cardboard to the required height. Cut the corners diagonally. Fold all overlap over card to inside, making sure the needlepoint is straight. I find using clothes pegs or bull dog clips excellent for this job. All overlap can be correctly positioned and held in place before finally taping or gluing. Position the trimmed card or heavy paper for the inside of the folder over the back of the front piece. Trim if necessary. Before gluing position one length each of ribbon halfway down front and back side edges, slipping 1" (2cm) of ribbon between folder and lining glue into position. Place folder opened out under a heavy object to dry overnight. Once dry on the inside of the folder gently score down the centre of the lining card to mark the spine. Fold in half and tie ribbons in a bow.

ROMANIAN GARDEN

For me the traditional woven rugs of Romania are like secret flower gardens. A quiet orderly border of either simple geometric shapes or a winding floral pattern encloses the garden like a garden wall. In the centre area the flowers appear to be randomly scattered and intertwined with stems and leaves, displaying their stylized petals in rich harmonious colours against a dark background. Sometimes mingled with these flowers, as though hiding in the garden, is a bird or animal.

Like the weavers of these rugs I too created my own secret garden using a mixture of geometric and floral patterns with beautiful deep colours that are typical of the Romanian rug.

R O M A N I A N   G A R D E N

Materials

Yarn

DMC tapestry wool in the following colours and approximate amounts.

Cushion

	7999	9	Skeins
	7501	10	Skeins
	7541	3	Skeins
	7302	1	Skein
	7202	1	Skein
	7759	1	Skein
	7758	1	Skein
	7167	1	Skein
	7356	2	Skeins
	7920	3	Skeins
	7273	1	Skein

Canvas

12-mesh single canvas 20" (50cm) square.

Finishing Materials

½yd (50cm) of backing fabric and matching thread. 14" (35cm) zip fastener. 65" (160cm) of piping cord or ready made cord for edging (optional). 15" (39cm) cushion pad.

Charted Design Area

185 stitches wide x 188 stitches high.

Finished Design

15½" (39cm) square.

Order Of Work

For full practical information on methods used in 'order of work', refer to Needlepoint Techniques (pages 144-55). Prepare the canvas. The entire design is worked in tent stitch using 1 strand of yarn throughout. Each square on the chart represents one stitch on the canvas. Following the chart, complete the design. Work background area last. Stretch the finished needlepoint before backing. Sew on cord if required.

The border pattern of this floral design is simple, quick to work and very effective. As with any border it defines the shape and size of a piece of needlepoint. Remember when adding a border that it should be planned from the centre of the length outwards towards each corner of the design. To adapt this border to fit a design or shape, such as a picture frame, one can either vary the number of border motifs or bring the motifs closer together by reducing the number of background stitches between each motif. This will give you a more condensed pattern.

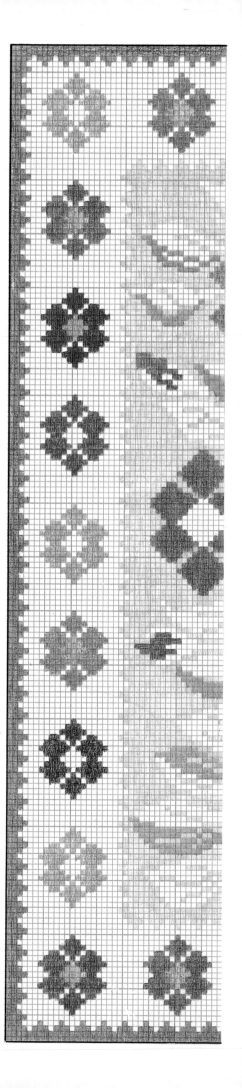

SCARLET GARDEN

During the last two centuries in Transylavania embroidered and woven patterns were worked in a predominance of red, black and blue, and consisted of various geometric forms, simplified birds and animals and an abundance of stylized flowers, two of which, the rose and the fern, I chose for my Scarlet Garden designs to reflect the love of flowers in folk art.

I wanted to use my designs in the way that Transylavanian women decorated their pillows and towels with areas of densely stitched pattern alternating with plain areas in one colour. My rose and fern designs are ideal if you feel daunted by working a whole needlepoint cushion. For a dramatic display I arranged these striking patterns with white lace cushions on a bed, reminiscent of the peasant's home on a festive occasion.

SCARLET GARDEN

Cushion: Rose Design

Materials

Yarn
DMC tapestry wool in the following colours and approximate amounts.

Colourway A
Cream background

Ecru	5	Skeins
7108	3	Skeins
7306	2	Skeins

Colourway B
Red background

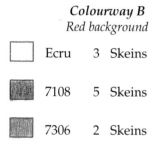

Ecru	3	Skeins
7108	5	Skeins
7306	2	Skeins

Canvas
12-mesh interlock canvas 8" (20cm) wide by 19" (48cm) high.

Finishing Materials
½yd (50cm) of finishing fabric and matching thread. 12" (30cm) zip fastener. Cord for edging (optional).

Charted Design Area
58 stitches wide x 180 rows high.

Finished Design
5" (13cm) wide x 15" (38cm) high.

Order Of Work
For full practical information on methods used in 'order of work', refer to Needlepoint Techniques

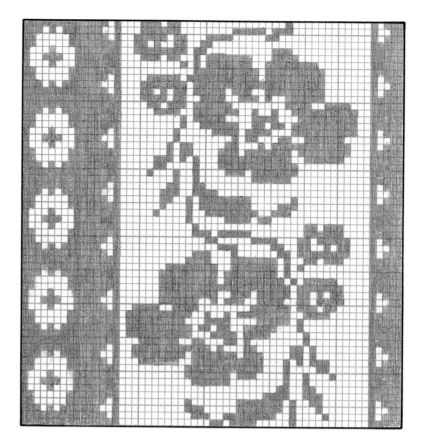

(pages 144-55). Prepare the canvas. The entire design is worked in tent stitch using 1 strand of yarn throughout. Each square on the chart represents one stitch on the canvas. Following the chart, complete the design, working in either colourway A, as given with the chart or in colourway B, by reversing all red and cream. Navy remains the same for both colourways. Stretch the finished needlepoint before making into a cushion.

For the front of the cushion, cut a piece of fabric the height of the needlepoint 15" (38cm) and the required width, depending on how wide you want the cushion. I chose a width of 10" (25cm), so I would finish with a square cushion. Add ⅝" (1.5cm) seam allowance. With right sides facing pin and tack fabric for cushion front to needlepoint along one side as close to the needlepoint as possible, using a small backstitch or a sewing machine. Back as for a standard needlepoint cushion. (See page 151). Sew on cord if required.

Cushion: Fern Design

Materials

Yarn
DMC tapestry wool in the following colours and approximate amounts

Ecru	5	Skeins
7108	7	Skeins
7306	2	Skeins

Canvas
12-mesh interlock canvas 16½" (42cm) square.

Finishing Materials
½yd (50cm) of finishing fabric and matching thread. 10" (25cm) zip fastener. Cord for edging (optional).

Charted Design Area
The completed design is 151 stitches wide by 153 stitches high.

Finished Design
12½" (32cm) square.

Order of work

For full practical information on methods used in 'order of work', refer to Needlepoint Techniques (pages 144-55). Prepare the canvas. The entire design is worked in tent stitch using 1 strand of yarn throughout. Each square on the chart represents one stitch on the canvas. Following the chart and referring to the photograph complete the design as follows: first work the larger central panel which is 79 stitches wide and 76 rows high. Repeat the height twice and then repeat the first row once more to give

you a height of 153 rows/stitches. On each side of this central pattern work border panels. Each side panel is 34 stitches wide and repeats every 38 rows. The left hand side panel is already set on the chart. For the right hand side reverse this pattern. For both side panels, repeat the pattern height four times and then repeat the first row once more (as for central panel). This will give you your correct height. Finally, work two rows in background colour only on either side, giving you a full width of 151 stitches.

Stretch the finished needlepoint

before making up into a cushion. For the front of the cushion, cut two pieces of fabric the height of the needlepoint, 12½ (32cm) and the required width, depending on how wide you want the cushion. I chose a width of 4" (10cm) for each border piece. Add ⅝" (1.5cm) seam allowance. With right side facing, pin and tack 1 piece of fabric each to either side of needlepoint (refer to photograph). Stitch as close as possible using a small backstitch or a sewing machine. Back as for a standard needlepoint cushion (see page 151). Sew on cord if required.

PENNSYLVANIAN SCROLL

When the early German settlers of Pennsylvania first began to decorate their furniture, they used motifs derived from early Germanic folk art. Popular motifs were flowers, in particular tulips, hearts, turtle doves, unicorns, all frequently framed by scroll patterns and all seen perhaps at their best on the lavishly painted dower or bridal chests. Common to almost all folk art cultures these chests contained an immense store of embroidered linen for the bride's trousseau. Some she would have spent most of her childhood making and some would have been inherited from her mother. To imitate the use of the scroll pattern as a border the picture frame seemed the ideal shape for translating a classic Pennsylvanian pattern into needlepoint.

PENNSYLVANIAN SCROLL

Materials

Yarn
DMC tapestry wool in the following colours and approximate amounts.

Frame

▨	7307	2	Skeins
▨	7304	8	Skeins
▨	7920	2	Skeins
☐	7491	2	Skeins

Canvas
12-mesh interlock canvas 17" (42.5cm) x 12½" (31cm).

Finishing Materials
Stiff cardboard. Masking tape.

Charted Design Area
165 stitches wide by 111 stitches high.

Finished Design
13¾" (34.5cm) x 9¼" (23cm).

Order Of Work
For full practical information on methods used in 'order of work', refer to Needlepoint Techniques (pages 144-55). Prepare the canvas. The entire design is worked in tent stitch using 1 strand of yarn throughout. Each square on the chart represents one stitch on the canvas. Following the chart, complete the design, working the background last. Stretch the finished needlepoint before making into a frame. (See page 153)

Unlike most of the border patterns in this book, this decorative scroll pattern is less adaptable as a cushion or rug edging. It has been designed to fit a particular shape and is not made up of a repeating motif, as for example the border of Romanian Garden (page 36) is. You could incorporate this pattern into a complete needlepoint piece, either working a pictorial subject or a geometric design in the centre and perhaps using the finished piece as a cover to a folder. (see Lover's Tulip page 32-5)

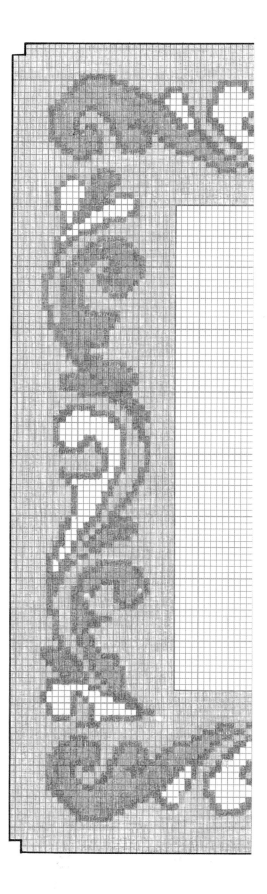

BAVARIAN STARS

The starting point for my Bavarian Stars design was a collection of jewelled coloured Easter eggs! All across central and eastern Europe women would in the weeks before Easter decorate eggs, using motifs familiar to them from weaving and embroidery. The egg surface was painted in a mosaic-like pattern of floral hearts, sun motifs, eight pointed stars and other geometric shapes.

It was this mosaic quality that I wanted to capture so I combined the traditional folk motifs of hearts and stars and broke some of them into segments with the random use of colour.

B A V A R I A N   S T A R S

Materials

Yarn
DMC tapestry wool in the following colours and approximate amounts.

Cushion

Colourway A
Red design

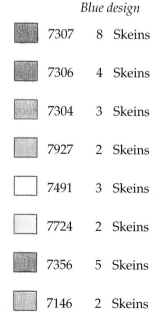

	7108	8	Skeins
	7209	5	Skeins
	7304	2	Skeins
	7724	2	Skeins
	Noir	5	Skeins
	7362	2	Skeins
	7421	1	Skein
	7337	1	Skein
	7491	1	Skein

Colourway B
Blue design

	7307	8	Skeins
	7306	4	Skeins
	7304	3	Skeins
	7927	2	Skeins
	7491	3	Skeins
	7724	2	Skeins
	7356	5	Skeins
	7146	2	Skeins

Canvas
12-mesh single canvas 19½" (49cm) square.

Finishing Materials
½yd (50cm) of backing fabric and matching thread. 12" (30cm) zip fastener. 61" (154cm) of piping cord or ready made cord for edging (optional). 15" (38cm) square cushion pad.

Charted Design Area
170 stitches square.

Finished Design
15" (38cm) square.

Order Of Work
For full practical information on methods used in 'order of work', refer to Needlepoint Techniques (pages 144-55). Prepare the canvas. The entire design is worked in tent stitch using 1 strand of yarn throughout. Each square on the chart represents one stitch on the canvas. Following the chart complete the design working in either colourway A, as given with the chart, or in colourway B, by referring to the photograph. Stretch the finished needlepoint before backing. Sew on cord if required.

This design offers numerous possibilities. Each diamond, containing either the heart or star motif, could be stitched as pin cushions making them ideal gifts or at the other end of the scale work squares of the complete design and join them together to make a rug (see Techniques page 153) which would look like a glorious patchwork. In addition, this design offers enormous scope for playing with colour as illustrated by the two colourways.

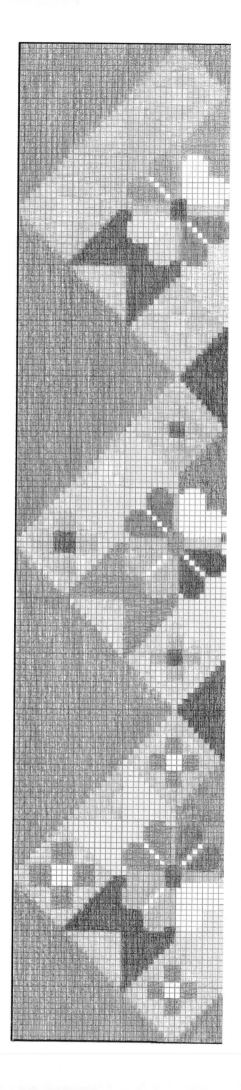

CHAPTER TWO

Home
and
Hearth

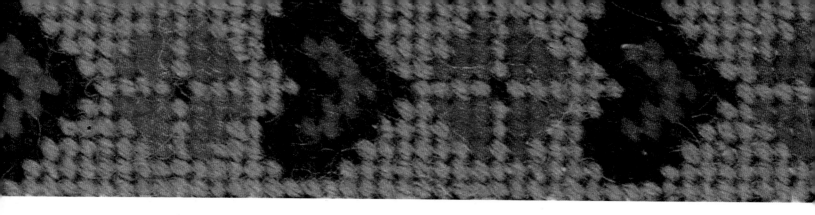

Unlike the other three chapters in this book which were inspired by popular patterns used in folk art, the starting point for this chapter was my fascination for the traditional peasant home from which this art flourished.

Although there are regional variations, the rustic nature and simplicity of folk interiors is common throughout rural homes, whether they be the timbered cabins found in the great valleys of Norway and Sweden, the stone dwellings scattered amongst the vineyards and gentle hills of Hungary, the Alpine chalets with their panoramic views, or even the clapboard farms of Pennsylvania. Their shapes make delightful and unusual motifs for needlepoint, as seen in my own design, Home Sweet Home.

The peasant home was built on a very simple plan with only a few small windows. Carpets, like curtains, were unknown in the early dwellings and there was little furniture, nothing more than the essentials. But what furniture there was, was patterned with carvings and paintings based on traditional motifs linked to deeply rooted customs. Sometimes, for example in Finland, these decorations were simple and unobtrusive using only soft colours, whilst others were lively and baroque in style, as frequently found on the food cupboards of Germany and Norway.

The peasants' rich imagination and inherent love of colour and pattern came into its own when it was lavished onto the great profusion of objects which were only brought out for

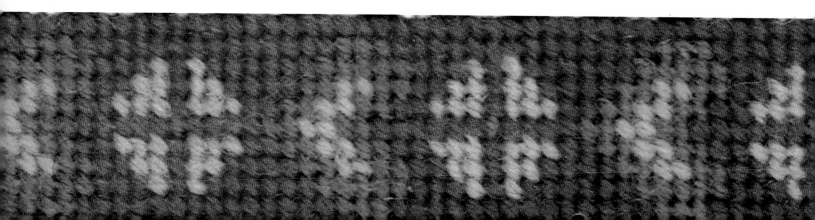

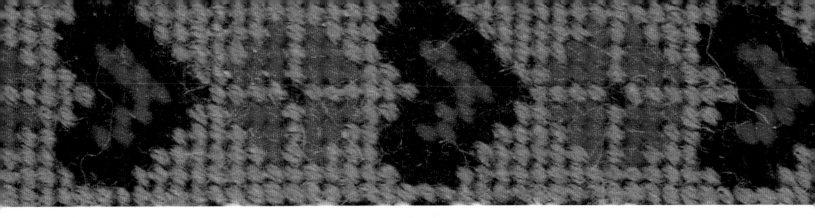

festivals and ceremonial occasions. Out of wooden chests came elaborately embroidered and woven hangings and covers to be hung on walls and rafters, or to be thrown across beds and benches. Sheets, pillow cases and towels were piled as high as possible to give the gaudiest appearance. (In Hungary women known for their skill in bedmaking were called in specially for this task!) Wooden racks ornamented with earthenware plates, mugs and tankards with lustrous glazed surfaces extended along the walls like a fresco to be admired. On these occasions floors were strewn with fine-cut twigs of fir or sometimes rye straw. Each interior became a riot of colour with every object playing a ritual role in the festivals.

This was not the only time the interior of the house was so gloriously decorated. When a girl had reached a marriageable age the larger or best room was specially prepared for her to receive her suitors. The most important part of a girl's dowry, the bed with the bedding piled as high as the ceiling, stood in the corner. Cushions, pillows and eiderdowns were covered in cases embroidered or woven in special decorative patterns, laden with symbolic meanings. Nothing was intended for practical use but rather as a display to signify that the mother had properly prepared her daughter for marriage. Why not decorate your own home with a display of needlepoint cushions. Don't restrict yourself to my patterns but create your own. Pick out household objects to incorporate into designs as I have done for my Hungarian Pot and Teatime patterns. And whatever your age splash out with the colour.

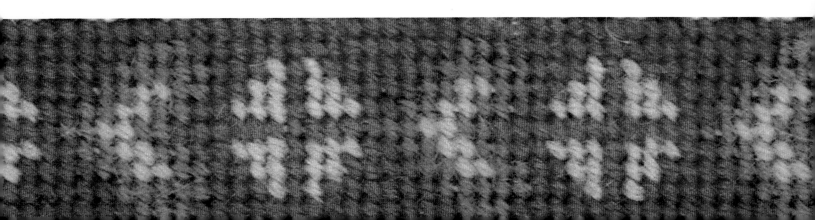

HUNGARIAN POT

Immersed in a secondhand bookshop I came across an illustrated volume of Hungarian folk textiles. What caught my eye immediately was a nineteenth-century breakfast tablecloth printed in indigo blue and white. It depicted a table laid ready for breakfast: a coffee pot, cups, plates cutlery and even rolls of bread. It was so striking and unusual that I was inspired to create my own table setting, also in shades of blue and cream. Focusing on lunch I laid my design with bowls and plates and a large serving pot all ready for twelve hungry guests.

HUNGARIAN POT

Materials

Yarn
DMC tapestry wool in the following colours and approximate amounts.

Cushion

Ecru	14	Skeins
7301	1	Skein
7323	1	Skein
7304	4	Skeins
7311	4	Skeins
7299	4	Skeins
7306	3	Skeins
7297	3	Skeins

Canvas
12-mesh single canvas 19" (47.5cm) square.

Finishing Materials
½yd (50cm) of backing fabric and matching thread. 12" (30cm) zip fastener. 61" (153cm) of piping cord or ready made cord for edging (optional). 15" (37cm) square cushion pad.

Charted Design Area
179 stitches wide by 179 stitches high.

Finished Design
15" (37.5cm) square.

Order Of Work
For full practical information on methods used in 'order of work', refer to Needlepoint Techniques (pages 144-55). Prepare the canvas. The entire design is worked in tent stitch using 1 strand of yarn throughout. Each square on the chart represents one stitch on the canvas. Following the chart, complete the design. Work the background last. Stretch the finished needlepoint before backing. Sew on cord if required.

The pot in the centre of this design would look very striking used on the top of a set of kitchen or dining room chairs. Why not depict a different utensil with each chair. One chair could have a casserole, another one a plate with knife and fork or maybe a coffee or tea pot. Instead of using this design as a cushion it would also look wonderful as a framed picture hanging in the kitchen surrounded by other blue and white china.

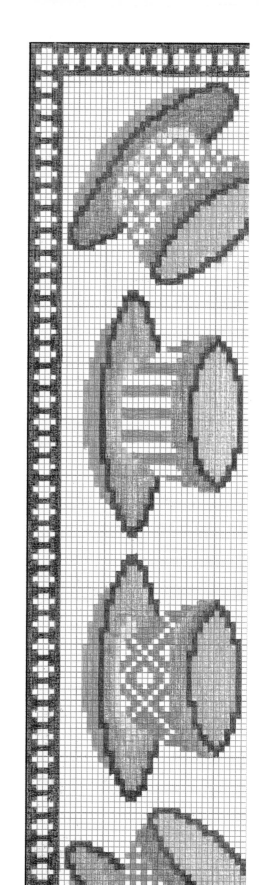

TEATIME

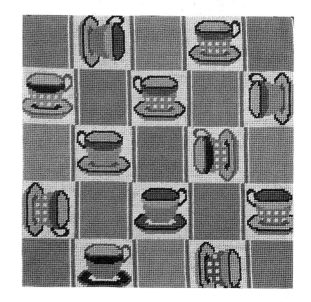

The amusing depiction of a table set with plates, cutlery, pots and even food which I found printed on the table cloths of nineteenth-century Hungary (and which inspired my Hungarian Pot design, page 62) I have since found also used on intricately painted and inlaid tables from Germany as well as on a unique nineteenth-century table cover from Pennsylvania. It was so heavily appliquéd and embroidered with plates, silverware and even a centrepiece of fruit that it was almost three dimensional.

For my design Teatime I continued with this folk theme of the set table, taking afternoon tea as my starting point. I chose the cup and saucer

as my main motif placing each one within a square of cream and arranging them in a chequerboard pattern, alternating each square with a block of solid colour. I was worried the design might look too regimented, so to create a sense of movement, I positioned the randomly coloured and patterned cups and saucers at different angles. For both my colourways, I chose bright colours, ones that lifted the spirit as an afternoon tea on a summers day might do. For the first, tones of blue with touches of sunshine yellow and for the second colourway, fresh greens with pink and terracotta, or even try it in shades of red and pink with hints of green.

TEATIME

Materials

Yarn
DMC tapestry wool in the following colours and approximate amounts.

Cushion

| | Colourway | |
	Blue design	
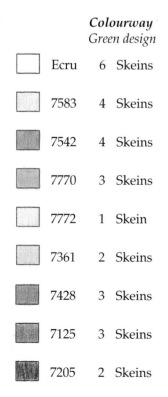 7301	1	Skein
7799	1	Skein
7798	3	Skeins
7996	4	Skeins
7314	4	Skeins
Ecru	6	Skeins
7297	2	Skeins
7473	4	Skeins

Cushion

| | Colourway | |
	Green design	
Ecru	6	Skeins
7583	4	Skeins
7542	4	Skeins
7770	3	Skeins
7772	1	Skein
7361	2	Skeins
7428	3	Skeins
7125	3	Skeins
7205	2	Skeins

Canvas
10-mesh single or interlock canvas 19" (48cm) square.

Finishing Materials
½yd (50cm) of backing fabric and matching thread. 12" (30cm) zip fastener. 63" (158cm) of piping cord or ready made cord for edging (optional). 15" (38cm) square cushion pad.

Charted Design Area
155 stitches high by 155 stitches wide.

Finished Design
15½" (39cm) square.

Order Of Work
For full practical information on methods used in 'order of work', refer to Needlepoint Techniques (pages 144-55). Prepare the canvas. The entire design is worked in tent stitch using 1 strand of yarn throughout. Each square on the chart represents one stitch on the canvas. Following the chart complete the design working in either colourway A, as given with the chart, or in colourway B, by referring to the photograph. Stretch the finished needlepoint before backing. Sew on cord if required.

A very pretty alternative use of this design would be as a placemat (see Alpine Check page 72). For a traditional rectangular placemat work a width of four pattern blocks (two plain blocks with stripes and two teacups) by a height of three pattern blocks. Whether you use one of my colourways or create your own combination, use the colours randomly and vary the position of each cup as I have done so each placemat will be different.

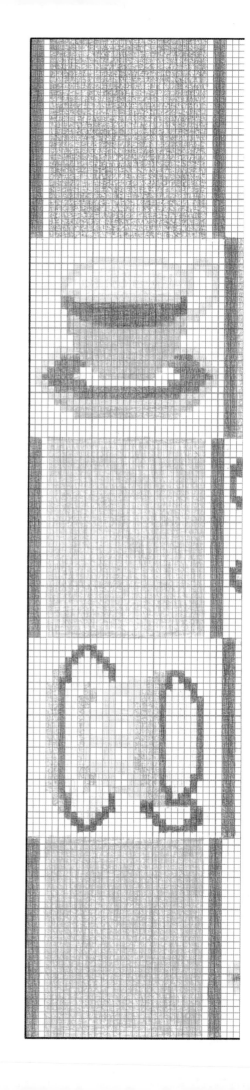

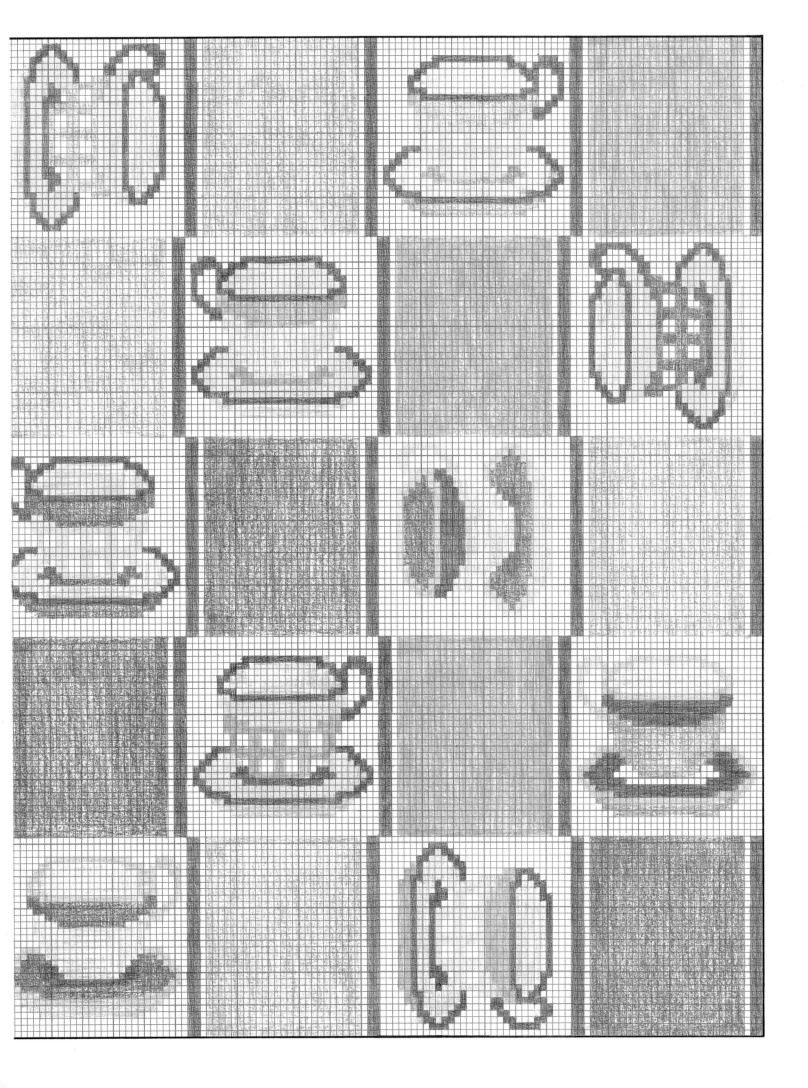

ALPINE CHECK

In the Alpine homes in the nineteenth century large dishes, plates, jugs and pots were traditionally patterned with naively painted figures or stylized garlands of flowers. Often simple linear decoration, as seen in my traditional Alpine Check design, was used to separate or frame areas of ornamentation, such as on the rim of a plate or round the neck of a vessel. A peasant woman took great pride in having as large a number of decorative plates and dishes as possible, displaying them on shelves and walls. Only on special occasions or for festivals would they be taken down and used. The acquisition of pottery was part of the long preparation for the wedding celebrations. These would sometimes start as soon as a child was born with the mother collecting plates and dishes so by the time the child was about fourteen years old she would have enough crockery to lay the table for the wedding feast.

Just as the peasant woman mixed and matched her dishes, so too can you with this check design. Checks have a classic appeal and they complement many different furnishing styles. They make excellent patterns for covering chairs seats and footstools, as well as borders to other needlepoint designs, particularly floral patterns. I have chosen just two colour schemes for my design but why not get out your crayons and have fun creating your own combinations.

ALPINE CHECK

Materials

Yarn
DMC tapestry wool in the following colours and approximate amounts.

Placemat

	7304	2	Skeins
	7362	2	Skeins
	7782	1	Skein
	7446	3	Skeins
	7759	3	Skeins
	Ecru	5	Skeins

Amounts below are for a square of repeating pattern. 87 x 87 stitches.

		Colourway A	Colourway B
		Red grid	*Blue grid*
	7304	2 Skeins	3 Skeins
	7362	1 Skein	1 Skein
	7782	1 Skein	1 Skein
	7446	1 Skein	1 Skein
	7759	3 Skeins	2 Skeins
	Ecru	3 Skeins	3 Skeins

Canvas
Placemat: 10-mesh interlock canvas 15" (37.5cm) x 10" (25cm).

Finishing Materials
Small amount of backing fabric.

Charted Design Area
Placemat: 121 stitches wide by 98 stitches high.

Finished Design
Placemat: 12" (30cm) x 10" (25cm).

Order Of Work
For full practical information methods used in 'order of work' refer to Needlepoint Techniques (pages 144-55). Prepare the canvas. The entire design is worked in tent stitch using 1 strand of yarn throughout. Each square on the chart represents one stitch on the canvas. Work a rectangle of 6 pattern squares wide by 5 pattern squares high (Refer to photograph). I chose to work only a border of Alpine Check, stitching the central area in the background colour, cream (Ecru) only. It might be equally nice to cover the whole placemat in the pattern or to design your own motif (floral, figurative, animal etc) to go in the centre with a border of Alpine Check. Complete the design, working in colourway A as given with the chart or in colourway B, by referring to the photograph. Work background area last. Stretch the finished needlepoint before backing. Back as for a cushion, omitting the zip fastener.

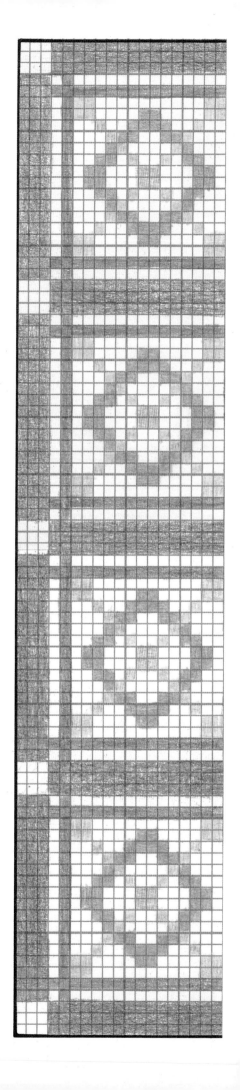

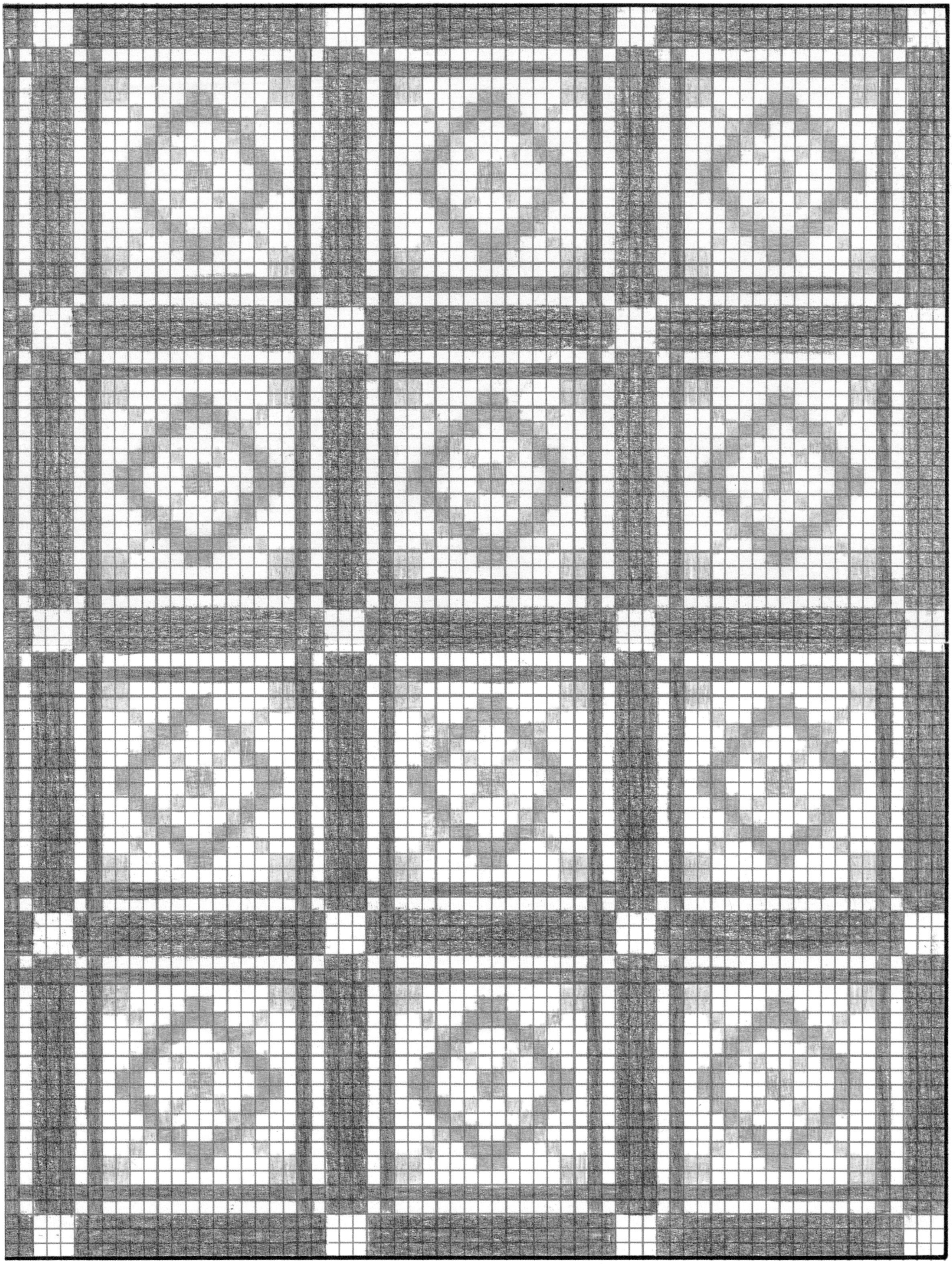

HOME–SWEET–HOME

I recently returned to the American Museum of Bath, which I had visited so regularly as a West country child, and looking amongst its fabulous collection of patchwork quilts and coverlets, I came upon this splendid house motif sewn into a bold nineteenth-century quilt from Pennsylvania. As with so many patterns in folk art its origin can no longer be identified. Like recipes, motifs were passed down from mother to daughter and circulated from one household to another and subtle variations crept in, each with a new name. The house motif composed of simple straight lines lends itself almost effortlessly to needlepoint design. In the spirit of a patchwork, I placed the houses in a grid of fences and coloured each one randomly, choosing the vivid colours of the early homesteads, such as venetian red, russet, pumkin yellow and blue grey.

HOME – SWEET – HOME

Materials

Yarn

DMC tapestry wool in the following colours and approximate amounts. (A = cream and B = black background)

Cushion					Frame	
Colourways	**A**	**B**				
Noir	2	8	Skeins	4	Skeins	
7432	3	3	Skeins	1	Skein	
7108	2	2	Skeins	1	Skein	
7920	3	3	Skeins	2	Skeins	
7491	8	2	Skeins	1	Skein	
7465	2	2	Skeins	1	Skein	
7361	2	2	Skeins	1	Skein	
7927	2	2	Skeins	1	Skein	
7326	2	2	Skeins	1	Skein	

Canvas

Cushion: 12-mesh interlock canvas 18" (45cm) square
Picture Frame: 12-mesh interlock canvas 15" (37cm) wide by 18" (45cm) high.

Finishing Materials

Cushion: ½yd (50cm) of backing, fabric and matching thread. 12" (30cm) zip fastener. 57" (143cm) of piping cord or ready made cord for edging (optional). 14" (35cm) square cushion pad.

Picture Frame: Stiff cardboard. Masking tape and glue.

Charted Design Area

Cushion: 170 stitches wide by 170 stitches high.
Picture Frame: 140 stitches wide by 174 stitches high.

Finished Design

Cushion: 14" (35cm) square.

Picture Frame: 11½" (29cm) wide by 14½" (36cm).

Order Of Work

Cushion: for full practical information on methods used in 'order of work', refer to Needlepoint Techniques (pages 144-55). Prepare the canvas. The entire design is worked in tent stitch using 1 strand of yarn throughout. Each square on the chart represents one stitch on the canvas. To complete the design in colourway A follow the chart exactly as given. For colourway B follow the chart but reverse all black (noir) and beige (7491). (Refer to the photograph). Stretch the finished needlepoint before backing. Sew on cord if required.

Frame: following the chart as given for the cushion and referring to the photograph work a rectangle of 5 houses and 4 fences high by 4 houses and 3 fences wide, leaving the central area of houses (3 houses high by 2 houses wide) unworked. Work further rows of stitches in background colour only all round inner edge, until, counting from inner edge of houses there are 5 rows of background colour. Repeat for outer edge, until counting from outer edge of houses there are 6 rows of background colour. Omit the 4 stitches at each corner. Stretch the finished needlepoint before making into a frame (See page 153).

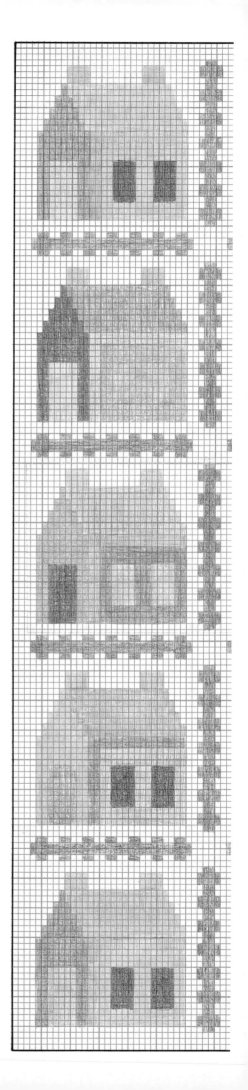

CHAPTER THREE

Lords
and
Ladies

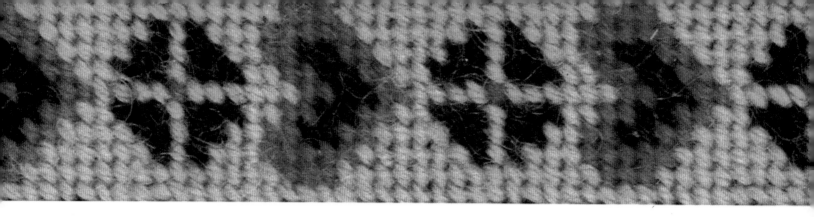

One of the joys of being a designer is discovering patterns that lead you on into a whole new world of unexplored images. For me the figures of folk art adapted and used as decorative motifs was one such world. These patterns were not purely for ornamentation but more importantly they were symbolic and were used on objects associated with a ritual or rite of passage.

In Russia and the Ukraine linen towels were embroidered with figurative motifs which depicted the earth goddess. These ceremonial towels were hung at crossroads from birch trees and in the home around icons and mirrors to fend off evil. In eastern Europe figurative motifs can be found embroidered or woven on the bed curtains which confined a mother and her baby for forty days after childbirth and protected her from illnesses and evil powers. The figures represented were female relations and neighbours shown in local peasant dress visiting and bringing food to the young mother.

The bridal pillow is another good example of the representation of figures in textile folk art. These pillows were richly embroidered with elaborate garlands of flowers framing a wedding couple, festively dressed and standing hand in hand under a big bridal crown. On the wedding day this pillow was placed on top of the marriage bed and became a symbol of honour and respect for the couple in their life to come. Furthermore the use of flowers was symbolic, ensuring the flourishing and well being of the family.

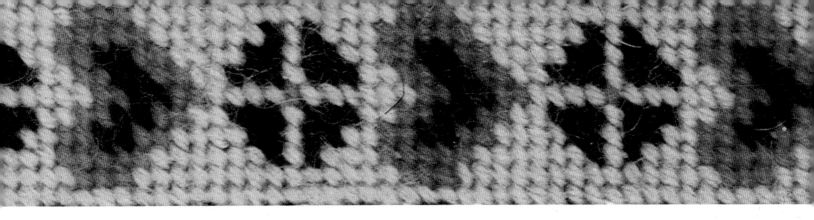

Biblical motifs in folk art were also common during the eighteenth and nineteenth centuries and reached their peak artistically in the unique wall hangings of Sweden. These paintings depicted scenes such as the parable of the wise and foolish virgins, the wedding at Cana, and the adoration of the Christ child by the three wise men. All the figures were depicted in the traditional costumes of the peasants of that time. Another popular biblical theme in folk art was that of Adam and Eve. The motif symbolized not only the promise of marriage, appearing on lover's gifts surrounded by small garlands of flowers and leaves but also as a symbol of the loving couple's good fortune in marriage.

In nineteenth-century Hungary, herdsmen and highwayman (known as betyars) were depicted on objects inlaid with sealing wax, idealized just as they were in the folk songs. The best examples are to be found on lids of mirror cases, weaving shuttles and the containers of razors. The pattern was first carved onto the surface of the object to be decorated and then coloured with sealing wax which was pressed into the grooves. You can see armed betyars fighting with gendarmes and herdsmen in festive garments, either alone with their flock, or with their sweet-hearts. If the loving couple were joined by a third figure, a musician, then they would be depicted dancing. Whether figures appear embroidered on a pair of gloves, relief-carved on a baking mould or painted on an earthenware jug, whether simple or elaborate, they all give an insight into folk culture as well as inspiring amusing designs for today.

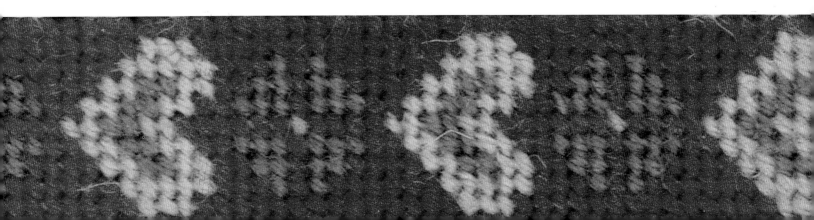

RIDE A COCK-HORSE

Both the Swedish Cavalier and Ride A Cock-Horse designs were inspired by the painted wall hangings of southern Sweden. These paintings, which were very long and sometimes extended the entire width of the room, began to replace the woven hangings that traditionally decorated the home in the eighteenth century. They were never used for everyday decoration, only for festivities when sometimes the interior of the room would resemble more the inside of a tent. After the celebrations the paintings were taken down, rolled up and stored in chests.

Most of these hangings depicted scenes from

biblical history with the holy figures dressed bizarrely in local costumes. Another popular subject and one that I explored for my two jolly horsemen, was that of a man, usually a farmer riding to a fair. Unlike the biblical paintings they usually had no special story to tell. Animals and hunting scenes were also depicted and flowers were used either decoratively to divide the scenes of a story or more frequently as a way of filling up empty spaces between the figures, a technique I used for both my designs. Rather than making cushions as I have done you could make your own wall hangings.

RIDE A COCK-HORSE

Materials

Yarn
DMC tapestry wool in the following colours and approximate amounts.

Cushion

■	7533	3	Skeins
■	7168	2	Skeins
■	7444	4	Skeins
□	7725	1	Skein
■	7781	1	Skein
■	7362	2	Skeins
■	7376	1	Skein
■	7398	1	Skein
■	7593	3	Skeins
■	7251	2	Skeins
□	Ecru	9	Skeins
□	7460	1	Skein
■	7950	1	Skein
■	7828	2	Skeins
□	7506	2	Skeins

Canvas
13-mesh single canvas 17" (43cm) x 18" (46cm).

Finishing Materials
½yd (50cm) of backing fabric and matching thread. 12" (30cm) zip fastener. 57" (140cm) of piping cord or ready made cord for edging (optional). Cushion pad 17" (43cm) x 18" (46cm).

Charted Design Area
178 stitches wide by 188 stitches high.

Finished Design
13½" (34cm) x 14½" (36cm).

Order Of Work
For full practical information on methods used in order of work, refer to Needlepoint Techniques (pages 144-55). Prepare the canvas. The entire design is worked in tent stitch using 1 strand of yarn throughout. Each square on the chart represents one stitch on the canvas. Following the chart, complete the design. Stretch the finished needlepoint before backing. Sew on cord if required.

This design is worked with a cream background but would look equally good with a dark background as though the rider was riding through the night. So as not to lose some of the coloured details against a dark background, for example the rider's hat and the horse's bridal, you could either change the colour of these details so they stand out or reverse all the cream (ecru) in the design with the dark brown (7533). You could also vary the colour of the horse from a chestnut into maybe a palamino by replacing the rust colours with a rich cream and a beige outline and then setting it against a night sky.

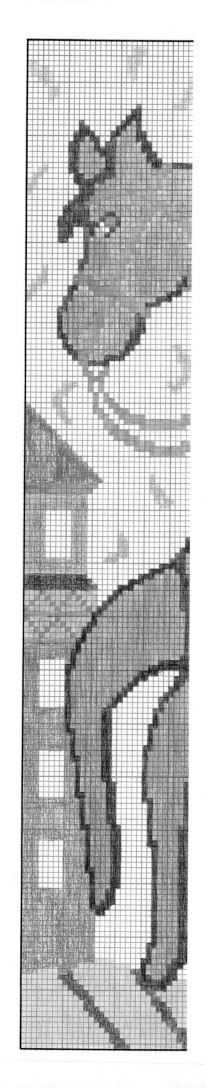

THE SWEDISH CAVALIER

Materials

Yarn
DMC tapestry wool in the following colours and approximate amounts.

Cushion

	Ecru	7	Skeins
	7533	2	Skeins
	7168	3	Skeins
	7444	3	Skeins
	7725	1	Skein
	7506	3	Skeins
	7781	1	Skein
	7362	3	Skeins
	7376	2	Skeins
	7398	1	Skein
	7598	3	Skeins
	7828	1	Skein
	7251	1	Skein
	7950	1	Skein
	7460	1	Skein

Canvas
13-mesh interlock canvas 18" (45cm) square.

Finishing Materials
½yd (50cm) of backing fabric and matching thread. 12" (30cm) zip fastener. 57" (140cm) of piping cord or ready made cord for edging (optional). 14" (35cm) square pad cushion.

Charted Design Area
179 stitches wide by 185 stitches high.

Finished Design
13" (34.5cm) x 14" (35.5cm).

Order Of Work
For full practical information on methods used in 'order of work', refer to Needlepoint Techniques (pages 144-55). Prepare the canvas. The entire design is worked in tent stitch using 1 strand of yarn throughout. Each square on the chart represents one stitch on the canvas. Following the chart, complete the design. Stretch the finished needlepoint before backing. Sew on cord if required.

The design hints given with the Ride A Cock-Horse pattern (page 92) also apply to the Swedish Cavalier pattern. In addition both designs would work well as framed pictures hanging on a nursery wall or in a child's bedroom.

LORD AND LADY WASHINGTON

This design was inspired by an eighteenth-century double portrait of George Washington and his wife. What particularly amused me about this bold painting was their scissor-like gestures, the details of the dress and the stylized branches of the plant.

Rather than inscribing my design with names as in the original painting I choose to stitch the year I completed the needlepoint. I have included charted numbers on page 98 so that you can adapt it to commemorate your own choice of occasion, maybe a wedding or an anniversary. This design would look equally good framed and hung on the wall.

LORD AND LADY WASHINGTON

Materials

Yarn
DMC tapestry wool in the following colours and approximate amounts.

Cushion

	7535	3	Skeins
	7510	3	Skeins
	7781	6	Skeins
	7147	2	Skeins
	7127	1	Skein
	7226	2	Skeins
	7196	2	Skeins
	7446	1	Skein
	7306	2	Skeins
	7363	1	Skein
	7326	1	Skein
	7169	2	Skeins

Canvas
12-mesh interlock canvas 15" (38cm) square.

Finishing Materials
½yd (50cm) of backing fabric and matching thread. 12" (30cm) zip fastener. 65" (162cm) of piping cord or ready made cord for edging (optional). 16" (41cm) square cushion pad.

Charted Design Area
143 stitches wide by 144 stitches high.

Finished Design
12" (30cm) square.

Order Of Work
For full practical information on methods used in 'order of work', refer to Needlepoint Techniques (pages 144-55). Prepare the canvas. The entire design is worked in tent stitch using 1 strand of yarn throughout. Each square on the chart represents one stitch on the canvas. Following the chart, complete the design. Work background last. Stretch the finished needlepoint before adding a fabric border (see pages 154) and backing. Sew on cord if required.

Below I have charted all the remaining numbers not used in my design so you can stitch your own dates.

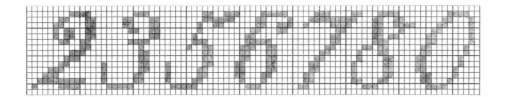

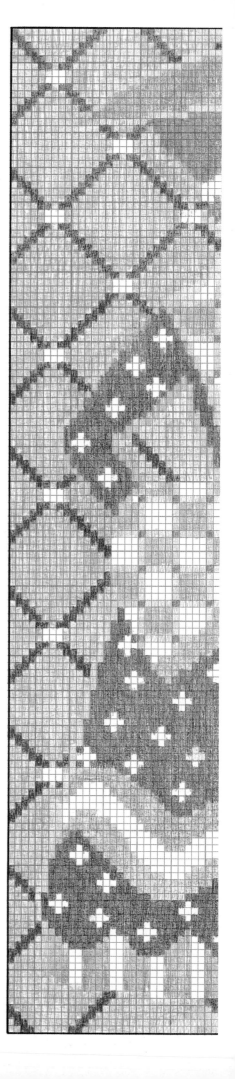

VILLAGE DANCE

The vivid colouring and rows of child-like figures that dance across this design are reminiscent of the heavily embroidered aprons from nineteenth-century Romania and will add a cheerful touch to any room. In Romania aprons were not worn to protect clothing but for ritual reasons. They were usually associated with marriage and declared a woman's new status. A bride, as well as changing her hairstyle and headdress, would change the style of apron she had worn as a child. Often the new apron would be carried through the streets in the wedding procession, hung from a pole like a flag above the bride for all to see.

VILLAGE DANCE

Materials

Yarn

DMC tapestry wool in the following colours and approximate amounts.

Cushion

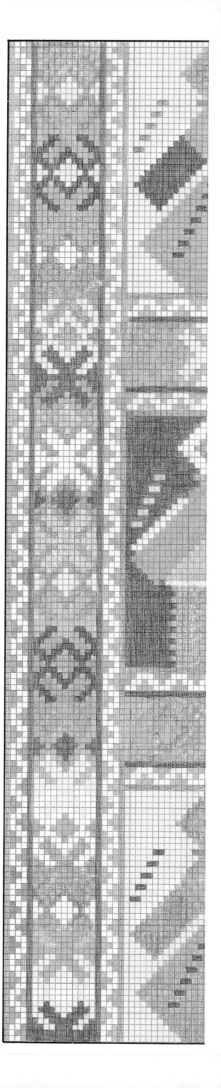	Noir	5	Skeins
	7107	7	Skeins
	7920	3	Skeins
	7782	5	Skeins
	7909	3	Skeins
	7316	4	Skeins
	Ecru	4	Skeins

Canvas

10-mesh single canvas 21" (52cm) square.

Finishing Materials

½yd (50cm) of backing fabric and matching thread. 14" (35cm) zip fastener. 69" (173cm) of piping cord or ready made cord for edging (optional). 17" (43cm) square cushion pad.

Charted Design Area

169 stitches wide by 171 stitches high.

Finished Design

17" (43cm) square.

Order Of Work

For full practical information on methods used in 'order of work', refer to Needlepoint Techniques (pages 144-55). Prepare the canvas. The entire design is worked in tent stitch using 1 strand of yarn throughout. Each square on the chart represents one stitch on the canvas. Following the chart, complete the design. Stretch the finished needlepoint before backing. Sew on cord if required.

This pattern can be used in any number of ways, the most obvious of which is using the rows of figures to decorate and trim a cushion in the same way I used my Scarlet Garden designs (page 45). To complete the needlepoint in this way choose a coloured fabric as near as possible to one of the colours in the design. The border design has a repeat of only 10 stitches which means that it could be used to edge practically any piece of needlepoint. If you find the colours I have chosen too bright you might prefer to try another colourway, for example, in the classic combination of different shades of blue with cream and maybe a hint of terracotta for contrast which would look wonderfully fresh.

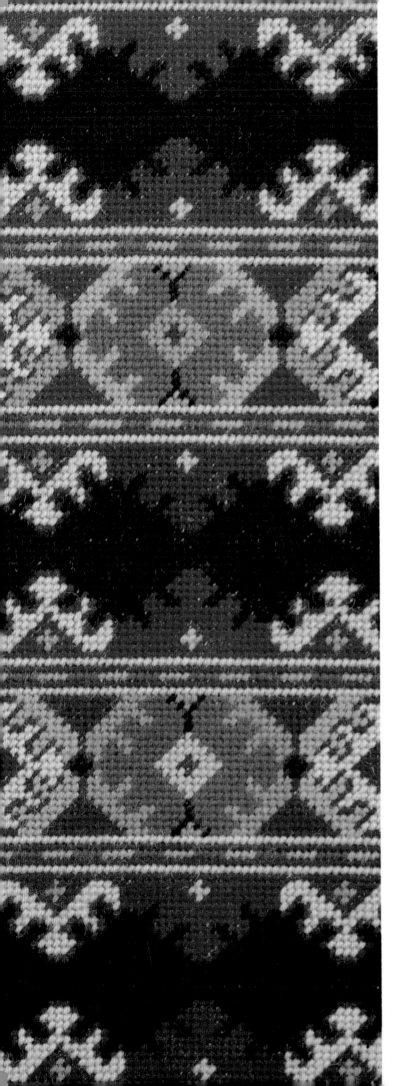

CHAPTER FOUR

Borders
and
Patterns

This chapter takes for its inspiration the breathtaking diversity of geometric patterns found within folk art, a world where no two designs are the same. They can be extended indefinitely and are ideal for making pieces of needlepoint of any size or shape, as you can see from my Norwegian Roses design (page 126) which was used both for a spectacle case and to cover a chair seat. Additionally they are excellent as border patterns defining a design just as a picture frame frames a picture.

Patterning of ordinary objects and tools was an intrinsic part of folk culture and it gave an object additional value as well as combining beauty and function. Traditionally, decorating was a task for women and girls and even male potters and furniture makers, who could quite easily decorate their products, usually left it to the womenfolk. Living in the creative atmosphere of the rural home a little girl watched from her earliest years her mother painting plates, embroidering shirts or working at the loom. If endowed with a greater talent than that of her mother or sisters the girl would add subtle variations to a design or pattern that she had learnt, often improving it, or she would originate her own designs.

Communal festivities were used as a sort of parade at which new decorations, in particular embroidered or woven designs, could be displayed. New innovations, however small, were quickly taken up and used by other women. Similarly new designs and techniques were also exchanged between villages, usually at festive gatherings. Sometimes girls were

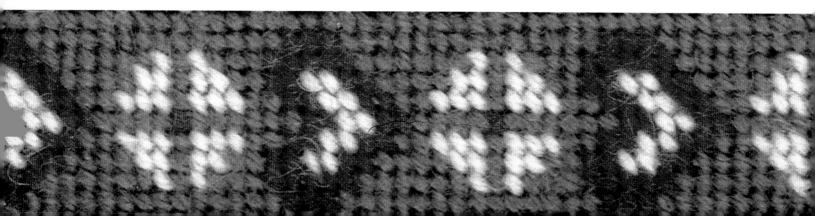

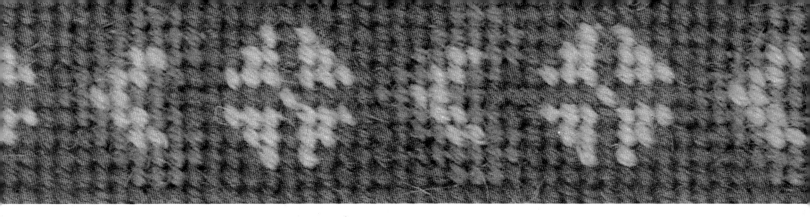

sent to other villages to learn to weave or embroider patterns that had been seen at local fairs or meetings. The more remote villages, cut off from the world by great rivers or treacherous mountains and thus not open to new patterns, developed the most individual style of decorating. But all new patterns wherever they came from were always used within the limits imposed by the traditions of the village.

And as old symbols were passed from mother to daughter and circulated from one household to another they were continually being simplified until they lost most of their original features and became instead a stylized shape. For example, an embroidered cross with a central spot was probably once a flower. The patterns which form such an integral part of peasant art once held a symbolic or magical meaning developed according to the beliefs and religion of the people. Today these designs are used purely for their decorative appeal.

One of the thrills for me when I look at traditional geometric patterns is that the design is effective both at a distance and at close range. Close to they are striking for their use of simple motifs, such as the triangle, zigzag, eight pointed star and cross and their colour harmony, and from afar the pattern is no longer distinguishable and the colours mingle. This is something I tried to recreate for some of my own designs, such as Cossack Jewels and Tyrolean Hearts. You can have a lot of fun with geometric patterns, particularly as they offer such enormous scope for playing with colour and can blend into most interiors.

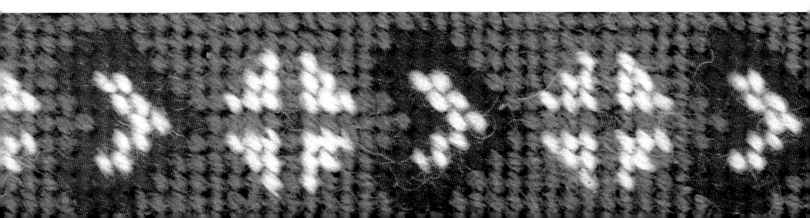

PRECIOUS PURSES

Many decorative objects in folk culture play an important part in certain customs, sometimes expressing intentions and emotions. Gifts given during courting stand for a confession of love as does a maypole decorated with ribbons and kerchiefs placed in front of a girl's house on the night preceding May Day. At a betrothal ceremony token gifts were exchanged to consecrate an engagement and just before the wedding a bride would present the groom with an elaborately embroidered wedding shirt which she herself had made along with a trousseau. Thinking of all these lovingly made gifts I was inspired to make my own. Little bags seemed ideal, perfect for the keeping of precious objects, the bearing of gifts or even as an evening bag.

PRECIOUS PURSES

Materials

Yarn
DMC tapestry wool in the following colours and approximate amounts.

Purse 1

		Colourway A Cream background	Colourway B Black background
	Ecru	4 Skeins	2 Skeins
	7108	2 Skeins	2 Skeins
	7767	2 Skeins	2 Skeins
	7742	1 Skein	1 Skein
	Noir	2 Skeins	4 Skeins

Purse 2

	Ecru	2 Skeins
	7108	2 Skeins

Canvas
12-mesh interlock canvas.
Purse 1: 10½" (26cm) square.
Purse 2: 10" (25cm) square.

Finishing Materials
Small amount of backing and lining fabric and matching thread.

Charted Design Area
Purse 1: 91 stitches wide by 91 stitches high.
Purse 2: 78 stitches wide by 78 stitches high.

Finished Design
Purse 1: 7½" (19cm) square.
Purse 2: 6½" (16.5cm) square.

Order Of Work
For full practical information on methods used in 'order of work' for both Purse 1 and Purse 2 refer to Needlepoint Techniques (pages 144-55). Prepare the canvas. Both designs are worked in tent stitch using 1 strand of yarn throughout. Each square on the chart represents one stitch on the canvas. For Purse 1, colourway A, complete the design, by following the chart exactly as given. For Purse 1, colourway B, complete the design by following the chart but reversing all black (noir) and cream (Ecru). All other colours remain the same. For both colourways work background area last. For Purse 2, follow the chart, repeating the pattern repeat of 26 stitches 9 times. Thus the purse will be 3 pattern repeats wide by 3 pattern repeats high. For a larger piece of needlepoint, repeat pattern until required size is achieved. For both designs stretch the finished needlepoint before making into purses.

Backing and lining a purse is a simple process and if you don't have a machine, hand stitching is equally effective. As with backing any piece of needlepoint choose a fabric that will enhance the design. The lining fabric should be thinner than the backing fabric. For small bags and purses I use left over pieces of dress lining.

For backing of purse cut one piece of fabric the area of the stretched needlepoint and add ⅝″ (1.5cm) seam allowance all round. With right sides

facing, pin and tack the needlepoint to the backing. Leaving the top edge open stitch as close as possible to the needlepoint edge using small stitches. Trim excess canvas and clip the corners diagonally. Turn purse right side out. Fold hem of needlepoint and backing to wrong side along top edge. Cut two pieces of lining the same size as the needlepoint and add ⅝″ (1.5cm) seam allowance. Join both pieces together, leaving top edge open. Clip corners diagonally to reduce bulk. Slip lining into purse or bag with wrong sides facing. Fold seam allowance of lining to wrong side and stitch neatly to needlepoint.

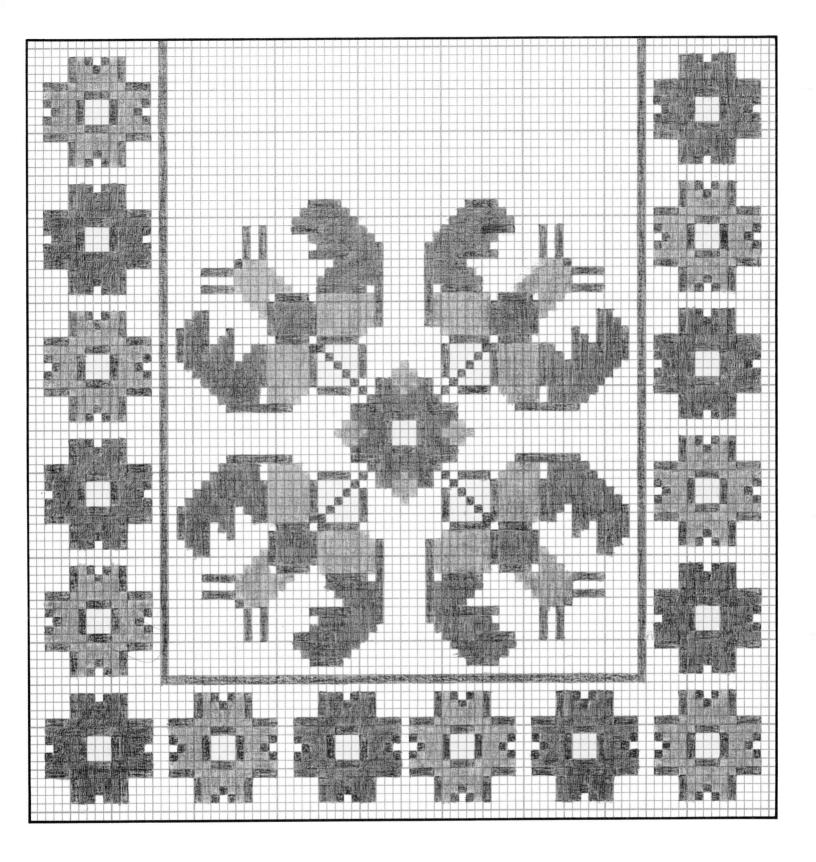

NORDIC SYMBOLS

A characteristic of almost all folk culture is the great variety of objects made of wood. In addition to furniture most domestic utensils used in the peasant home were wooden: drinking vessels, butter and cake stamps, cheese molds, weaving implements and containers of all sizes. These utensils were frequently decorated with carved or burned in designs. As with most folk ornamentation the choice of pattern was always influenced by the shape of the object. This was so with my picture frames. I needed simple motifs that would work not only as repeat patterns but also with limited colours. Snowflakes, diamonds and abstracted flowers were ideal.

NORDIC SYMBOLS

Materials

Yarn

DMC tapestry wool in the following colours and approximate amounts.

Picture Frame 1

▨	7920	7	Skeins
☐	Ecru	5	Skeins

Picture Frame 2

☐	Ecru	3	Skeins
▨	7920	3	Skeins
▨	7304	2	Skeins
▨	7363	1	Skein

Picture Frame 3

☐	Ecru	3	Skeins
▨	7920	2	Skeins
▨	7304	4	Skeins

Picture Frame 4

☐	Ecru	4	Skeins
▨	7920	3	Skeins
▨	7304	2	Skeins

Canvas

12-mesh interlock canvas.

Picture Frame 1: 12½" (31cm) x 15" (37cm).

Picture Frame 2: 12" (30cm) x 12" (30cm).

Picture Frame 3: 10½" (26cm) x 11" (29cm).

Picture Frame 4: 12" (30cm) x 12" (30cm).

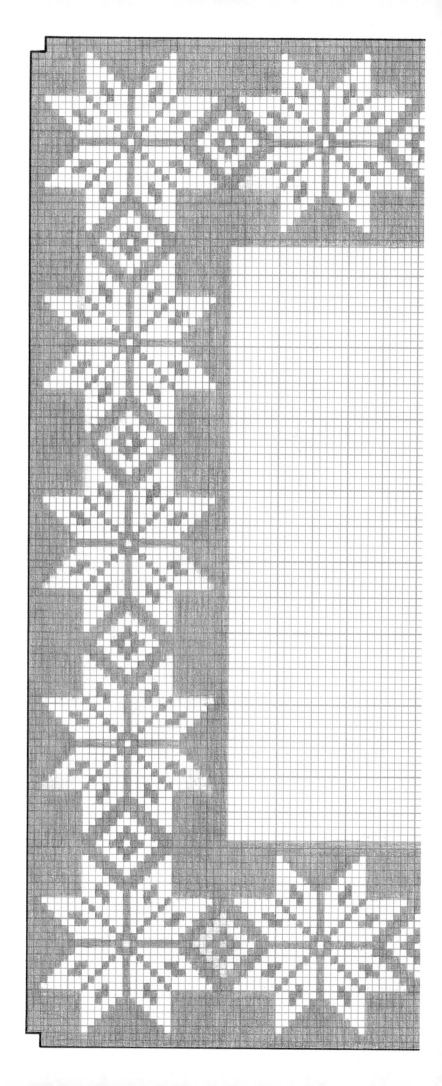

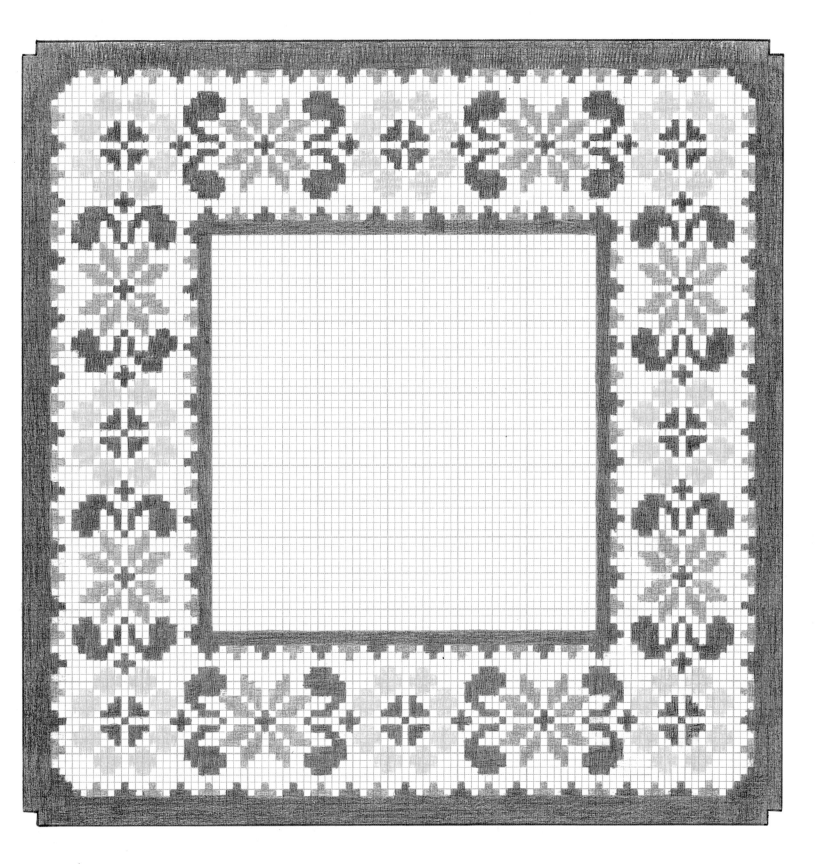

Finishing Materials
Stiff cardboard. Masking tape.

Charted Design Area
Picture Frame 1: 113 stitches wide by 141 stitches high.

Picture Frame 2: 109 stitches wide by 109 stitches high.

Picture Frame 3: 87 stitches wide by 103 stitches high.

Picture Frame 4: 109 stitches wide by 109 stitches high.

Finished Design
Picture Frame 1: 9½" (23.5cm) x 11¾" (29.5cm).

Picture Frame 2: 9" (22.5cm) x 9" (22.5cm).

Picture Frame 3: 7¼" (18cm) x 8½" (21.5cm).

Picture Frame 4: 9" (22.5cm) x 9" (22.5cm).

Order of Work
Order of work is the same for all four picture frames. For full practical information methods used in order of work, refer to Needlepoint Techniques (pages 144-55). Prepare the canvas. The entire design is worked in tent stitch using 1 strand of yarn throughout. Each square on the chart represents one stitch on the canvas. For picture frames 1 and 3 only one half of each frame is given. For picture frame 1 following the chart, complete one half of the frame (57 stitches). Repeat once more for other half, reversing pattern and omitting the first vertical row of stitches in centre of frame (56 stitches). This will give you a total width of 113 stitches. For picture frame 3 complete as for picture frame 1, working 44 stitches from chart and then 43 stitches for other side of frame for a total width of 87 stitches. For picture frames 2 and 4 following the chart, complete the design. For all frames work background last. Stretch the finished needlepoint before making into a frame (See page 153).

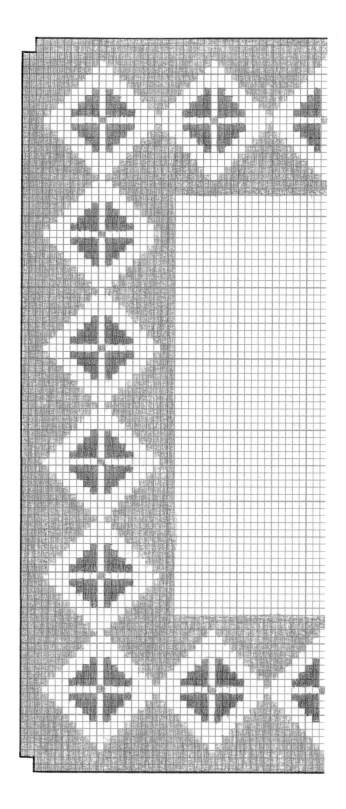

TYROLEAN SYMBOLS

The timbered Tyrolean houses to be found in the Austrian Alps were sparsely furnished during the eighteenth and nineteenth centuries. The rustic nature and simple style of the interior was typical of nearly all folk homes but the Tyrolese excelled in carving and frequently decorated their sturdy furniture with traditional designs using either chip carving, or openwork as was commonly seen on the backs of chairs. One of the most extensively used motifs was the symbol of the heart. For this design I chose it as my repeating motif and then in keeping with Tyrolean traditions I combined the hearts with flowers by working a border of flower heads.

T Y R O L E A N   H E A R T S

Materials

Yarn
DMC tapestry wool in the following colours and approximate amounts.

Cushion

Colourway A
Red border

	Noir	6	Skeins
	7107	6	Skeins
	7920	4	Skeins
	7782	4	Skeins
	7320	4	Skeins
	Ecru	4	Skeins

Cushion

Colourway B
Blue border

	7690	5	Skeins
	Noir	4	Skeins
	7491	2	Skeins
	7127	3	Skeins
	7226	2	Skeins
	7198	4	Skeins
	7781	2	Skeins
	7363	2	Skeins
	7255	2	Skeins

Canvas
10-mesh single canvas or interlock 20" (50cm) square.

Finishing Materials
½yd (50cm) of backing fabric and matching thread. 14" (35cm) zip fastener. 65" (163cm) of piping cord or ready made cord for edging (optional). 16" (40cm) square cushion pad.

Charted Design Area
159 stitches wide by 159 stitches high.

Finished Design
16" (40cm) square.

Order Of Work
For full practical information on methods used in 'order of work', refer to Needlepoint Techniques (pages 144-55). Prepare the canvas. The entire design is worked in tent stitch using 1 strand of yarn throughout. Each square on the chart represents one stitch on the canvas. Following the chart, complete the design, working in either colourway A as given with the chart, or in colourway B by referring to the photograph. Stretch the finished needlepoint before making into a frame. (See page 153)

The simple repeating heart pattern to be found in the centre of this design would look very effective used for bags and purses (for examples see Cossack Jewels page 134-43) and worked in the original bright colours they would have a strong Christmas feel.

The heart pattern could also be extended to fit any piece of furniture but because it is a relatively small pattern and could look proportionally wrong I would recommend enlarging the design. The easiest way to double the size of the pattern is to use a 7-mesh canvas and the yarn double. Wonderfully quick and easy!

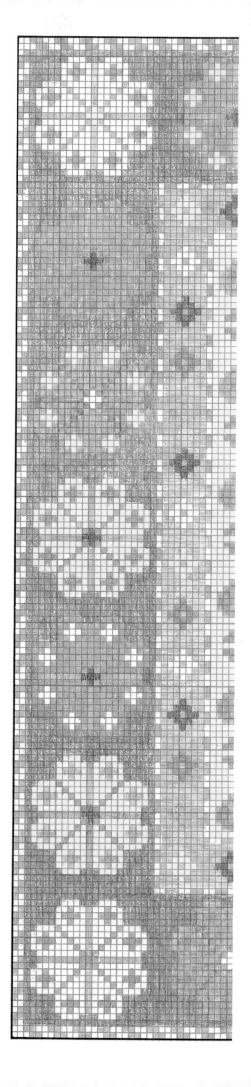

NORWEGIAN ROSES

It is colour that so often gives me a lust for designing and is the starting point for a new piece of work. This was so for my Norwegian Roses. It was the pure, bright hues of the vivid but harmonious rose paintings of Norway that were my inspiration.

The tradition of rose painting started at the beginning of the eighteenth century and developed into a type of rural flower painting with local masters (who had no formal training) travelling from farm to farm, often spending months and months in one place carving and painting not only furniture and utensils but also magnificent interiors. Wall paintings replaced the earlier woven wall hangings and were a way for farmers and peasants to express new-found prosperity. The name arose from the artists favourite motif, the rose, although other flowers and leaves were used as well as occasional figures and religious scenes.

Thinking of all this colour I particularly wanted to create a simple pattern because it

NORWEGIAN ROSES

would allow me not only endless design possibilities but also an inexhaustible scope for playing with colour. So I chose as my main motif the rosette, an abstract flower head, not only because it felt in keeping with the theme of rose painting but also because it is one of the most frequently used flower motifs in folk culture. I worked with two very different colourways. For the first, seen covering a chair on page 127, the traditional colours of the rose painting, and in complete contrast for the spectacle case opposite stronger, more classic colours.

NORWEGIAN ROSES

Materials

Yarn

DMC tapestry wool in the following colours and approximate amounts.

Chair

7306	2	Skeins
7304	7	Skeins
7920	4	Skeins
7446	5	Skeins
7362	4	Skeins
7473	3	Skeins
7759	5	Skeins
7491	6	Skeins

Spectacle Case

Noir	1	Skein
7797	4	Skeins
7909	2	Skeins
7920	2	Skeins
Ecru	2	Skeins

Canvas

Chair: 10-mesh single canvas. See 'order of work' below for measurements.

Spectacle case: 12-mesh interlock canvas 10" (25cm) wide x 11" (27cm) high.

Finishing Materials

Spectacle case: small amount of lining fabric and matching thread.

Charted Design Area

Chair: A repeat pattern of 191 stitches wide by 72 stitches high.

Spectacle Case: 84 stitches wide by 91 stitches.

Finished design

Chair: the repeat I worked with as given with the chart is 19" (47.5cm) wide by 7" (18cm) high. Finished design depends on size of area being stitched.

Spectacle Case: 7" (17.5cm) x 7½" (19cm).

Order Of Work

Chair seat: To extend pattern over a chair seat as I have done, or any other piece of furniture, measure area to be covered and add at least a 2" (5cm) margin all round. For full practical information on methods used in order of work, refer to Needlepoint Techniques (pages 144-55). Prepare the canvas. Calculate the pattern repeat to fit symmetrically across the area of canvas to be stitched. The entire design is worked in tent stitch. Each square on the chart represents one stitch on the canvas. Following the chart complete the design working the background colour to each stripe last. Stretch the finished needlepoint before upholstering.

Spectacle Case: As for chair seat, for full practical information on methods used in 'order of work' refer to Needlepoint Techniques (pages 144-55) Prepare the canvas. The entire design is worked in tent stitch. Each square on the chart represents

one stitch on the canvas. Referring to the photograph for colour arrangement and to the chart for pattern, work four rows of medallions for width of design (84 stitches), i.e. two rows for each side of case. For height repeat medallion motif five times plus one row of stitches in background colour to create a total of 91 stitches. Stretch the finished needlepoint before trimming the excess canvas to ½" (1cm). Fold hem to wrong side along top and bottom edges. Cut lining the same size as the needlepoint adding ½" (1cm) seam allowance. Fold seam allowance to wrong side, press and pin to needlepoint. Stitch neatly to needlepoint. Fold needlepoint in half lengthways with wrong sides together and join seams using tent stitch.

Instead of placing the rose motif on
coloured vertical stripes, as I have done,
you might like to try diagonal or
horizontal stripes, even blocks of colour
to create a patchwork effect, or for a far
simpler pattern you could work all the
roses on a single coloured background. I
have used only one motif throughout this
design but why not introduce different
motifs: other abstract flowers,
snowflakes, hearts, even numbers and
letters. The most obvious use of this
pattern in addition to the two ways I
have used it is as a border pattern
framing a design.

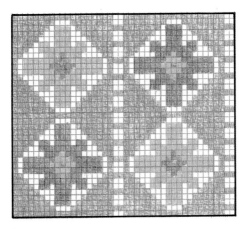

COSSACK JEWELS

For a long time I associated Russian textiles with spectacular ecclesiastical embroideries, opulent brocades and clothing from the Imperial household. It was whilst researching these designs that I first discovered for myself the folk embroideries of Russia. Clothing, headdresses, tablecloths, ceremonial towels carried at weddings and other religious and family occasions all ornamented with embroidery, remarkable not only for the richness of its colour schemes but also for the immensely elaborate designs. It was like discovering jewels.

COSSACK JEWELS

As with most folk cultures, from Russia across to Western Europe and up into Scandinavia, embroidery on clothing was not just for ornamentation but also to protect the wearer from evil spirits and physical harm. Spirits were kept out by decorating every opening and edge. Embroidery was commonly placed encircling the neck, along hems and cuffs, around pockets and at buttonholes. Areas of clothing that covered the vulnerable parts of the body were the most heavily embroidered. If the pattern was repeated its force was said to be strengthened.

Colour was also used for protection, with red being the most predominant and powerful colour in peasant embroidery.

In Russia costumes were decorated with patterns which were frequently geometric, ranging from simple motifs to complex multiple designs, like those seen in a kaleidoscope as a child and were derived from unique and deeply rooted local traditions: the cross, triangles, stars, zigzags, squares and plain and toothed diamonds were all important motifs combined in countless variations of repeating patterns.

COSSACK JEWELS

Materials

Yarn
DMC tapestry wool in the following colours and approximate amounts.

Design 1 — Bag

	Noir	3	Skeins
	7107	2	Skeins
	7911	2	Skeins
	7782	1	Skein
	Ecru	1	Skein

Design 2 — Bag

	Noir	1	Skein
	7107	5	Skeins
	7911	3	Skeins
	7782	2	Skeins
	Ecru	2	Skeins

Design 3 — Bag

	Noir	3	Skeins
	7107	3	Skeins
	7920	2	Skeins
	7782	3	Skeins
	7583	2	Skeins

Design 4

		Bag		Footstool	
	Noir	2	Skeins	5	Skeins
	Ecru	1	Skein	2	Skeins
	7782	2	Skeins	2	Skeins
	7920	2	Skeins	4	Skeins
	7107	1	Skein	4	Skeins
	7911	1	Skein	2	Skeins

Design 5 — Bag

	Ecru	5	Skeins
	Noir	2	Skeins
	7107	5	Skeins
	7782	1	Skein
	7583	1	Skein

Chair

		Seat		Back	
	Noir	8	Skeins	4	Skeins
	7492	6	Skeins	3	Skeins
	7110	6	Skeins	2	Skeins
	7920	3	Skeins	1	Skein
	7363	2	Skeins	2	Skeins
	7108	6	Skeins	3	Skeins
	7506	3	Skeins	2	Skeins

Design 1

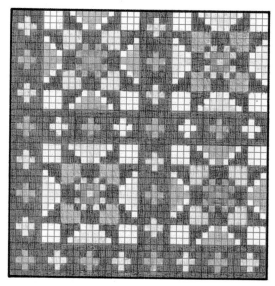

Design 2

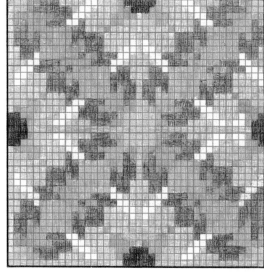

Design 4

Canvas

For bags: 10-mesh interlock canvas.

For footstool and chair: 10-mesh interlock or single canvas.

Design 1

Bag: 11" (28cm) square.

Design 2

Bag: 12" (30cm) square.

Design 3

Bag: 11" (28cm) x 13" (32cm).

Design 4

Bag: 11" (28cm) square.

Footstool: 18" (45cm) square.

Design 5.

Bag: 11" (28cm) x 12" (30cm).

Chair seat: 23" (58cm) x 20" (50cm).

Chair back: 23" (58cm) x 11" (28cm).

Finishing Materials

For all bags a small amount of backing and lining fabric matching thread.

For footstool: upholstery tacks.

For chair: ¾ yard (80cm) of backing fabric and matching thread.

Charted Design Area

Design 1

Bag: 81 stitches wide by 81 stitches high.

Design 2

Bag: 85 stitches wide by 81 stitches high.

Design 3

Bag: 95 stitches wide by 121 stitches high.

Design 4

Bag: 81 stitches wide by 81 stitches high.

Footstool: 141 stitches wide by 141 stitches high at widest points (across diameter).

Design 5

Bag: 97 stitches wide by 112 stitches high.

Design 6

Chair seat: 185 stitches wide by 155 stitches high.

Chair back: 185 stitches wide by 155 stitches high.

Finished Design

Design 1

Bag: 8" (20cm) square.

Design 3

Design 2

Bag: 8½" (21cm) square.

Design 3

Bag: 8" (20cm) x 10" (25cm).

Design 4

Bag: 8" (20cm) square.

Footstool: 14" (35cm) diameter.

Design 5
Bag: 8" (20cm) x 9" (23cm)
Chair seat: 18" (46cm) x 15" (39cm)
Chair back: 18" (46cm) x 7" (17cm).

Order Of Work
Bags
For full practical information on methods used in 'order of work' refer to Needlepoint Techniques (pages 144-55). Prepare the canvas. For each bag the entire design is worked in tent stitch using 1 strand of yarn throughout. Each square on the chart represents one stitch on the canvas. Each chart gives one complete pattern repeat. This can be repeated as many times as you wish depending on size of needlepoint required. For each bag 1 worked each repeat as follows, always starting the first repeat in the top left hand corner of canvas. Remember to leave margin.

For design 1 following the chart, work the pattern repeat of 40 stitches by 40 stitches 4 times. Thus the bag will be 2 pattern repeats wide by 2 pattern repeats high. (Refer to photograph).

For design 2 following the chart, work the 'pattern repeat' of 40 stitches by 40 stitches 4 times. Thus the bag will be 2 pattern repeats wide by 2 pattern repeats high. Complete bag by repeating 5 rows/stitches of grid part of pattern along bottom and right side edge of bag. (This is so the pattern in symmetrical).

For design 3, following the chart first work the wider central panel of pattern down the middle of your canvas. On either side of this panel work the outer pattern panels for which the left hand panel is already set on the chart. Repeat for right (refer to photograph).

For design 4, following the chart work the pattern repeat of 40 stitches by 40 stitches 4 times. Thus the bag will be 2 pattern repeats wide by 2 pattern repeats wide by 2 pattern repeats high. (Refer to photograph).

For design 5, following the chart, first work the narrower central panel of pattern down the middle of your canvas. On either side of this panel work the outer panels, the right-hand panel is already set on the chart. Repeat for left (refer to photograph). Stretch all bags before backing and lining (See page 154).

The directors chair (page 137) illustrates beautifully how a repeat pattern can be extended to cover a piece of furniture. I used design 5.

Footstool
Prepare the canvas, clearly marking the outside

Design 5

dimensions of the whole design area. Following the chart for pattern 4, begin in the centre of the canvas with the centre of the pattern repeat and then work outwards repeating the pattern until it extends to your marked outside edges. Stretch the finished needlepoint. Evenly position needlepoint over footstool to be covered. Tack down the edges, pulling the needlepoint tight across the stool and positioning upholstery tacks as near as possible to the edges of the design. Cut excess canvas.

Techniques

Canvas

There are three different types of canvas: single-thread (or mono), interlock and double-thread (or Penelope).

Single thread canvas is evenly woven using single threads. It is particularly strong and sturdy. Interlock canvas looks similar to single thread canvas, but instead of the threads passing under and over one another, the threads are twisted so that they lock at the intersection, thus preventing the canvas threads shifting with the tension of the stitches or from fraying around the edges. Double-thread canvas is woven using pairs of threads, and stitches are normally worked over both threads. However, by separating the pairs and stitching over one thread only, much finer stitches can be worked. This canvas is ideal for designs where more than one type of stitch is used. Fine stitches used for detail can be combined on the same canvas with larger background stitches. Double-thread canvas can be confusing to work with, so it would not be my first choice for a beginner.

Most canvas is woven from cotton or linen and except for interlock canvas comes in a choice of three colours; white, the most readily available, Ecru, an off white colour and antique, a brown colour (which is actually unbleached canvas). Interlock is only made in white and therefore far more care has to be taken to cover the canvas well with the stitches to prevent any harsh white threads showing through. For this reason I tend to use interlock canvas more for those designs with a pale background colour (e.g. Baltimore Fruits, colourway A, page 26).

Apart from coming in different types and colours,

The three different types of canvas - single, interlock and double-thread.

canvas comes in a range of sizes, measured by the number of threads or holes per 1" (2.5cm). This is known as the mesh count. Canvas can come as fine as 32 threads or holes per 1" (2.5cm), making it ideal for petit-point, or as coarse as 3 threads per 1" (2.5cm) and used for needlepoint rugs. I generally like using a medium mesh size of 10 or 12 holes to the 1" (2.5cm). It is fine enough to create good detail and is perfect for tent stitch.

The choice of canvas is a matter of personal taste. Be careful with interlock canvas. Unless it is firmly framed during work, it will tend to pull out of shape. Being so fine and pliable it can then be difficult to stretch back, as the canvas will not take a lot of tension without breaking. I prefer to use interlock for my smaller pieces of work (e.g., picture frames, bags, spectacle cases).

When buying canvas, try to buy the best quality you can afford and always buy sufficient to allow at least a 2" (5cm) margin around the finished design.

Yarns

There are three standard needlepoint yarns available. Crewel, tapestry and Persian. Crewel yarn is fine, twisted 2-ply yarn and several strands together are needed to cover 10 to 13-mesh canvas.

Tapestry wool is thicker than crewel and a single strand will cover 10 to 13-mesh canvas whilst two strands together will cover a 7-mesh canvas. Persian yarn is made up of three strands and like crewel yarn, the strands can be easily separated giving the flexibility to use the same yarn on different gauges of canvas as well as to do a variety of stitches on one canvas. In addition, you can mix your own colours by using two or three different coloured strands and threading all together into the one needle. For the purpose of this book, mixing colours and separating strands is not required and for that reason my preference was for tapestry wool.

Whichever yarn you finally choose to use it is essential that the yarn is thick enough to cover the canvas thread completely but not so thick as to create difficulty in passing the threaded needle through the canvas which results in distorting the canvas weave.

When buying yarns for the needlepoint designs in this book, remember that amounts given are only approximate. Amounts of yarn used do vary enormously from one person to another depending how loosely or tightly you work. If possible buy all yarn at one time, particularly yarn for a background or large area worked in one colour. If not possible keep a record of the dye lot so you can match the colour exactly.

If you wish to duplicate my needlepoint designs exactly as given in this book buy the same brand of tapestry wool - DMC, and the same colour number as given with each design. If you wish to substitute yarns of another brand, use the conversion chart at the back of the book. The conversion chart is a list of all the DMC shades used in this book with each shade followed by the nearest equivalent colour available in brands. Appleton, Anchor and Paterna (all readily available). But please note, yarn colours vary from brand to brand, so if you do use an alternative yarn the finished result will not be exactly the same as my original.

Needles

Tapestry needles have large eyes and a rounded point so as not to split the canvas. They are available in a range of sizes from 13 to 26, the higher the number the smaller the needle. It is important that the eye of the needle is sufficiently large to allow the yarn to pass through easily without fraying. In addition, the threaded needle must not be too thick to pass through the canvas, otherwise the canvas threads will be displaced. As a general guide, I use size 18 for a 10 and 12-mesh canvas.

Frames

When working on a small canvas it is possible to hold the canvas in one hand while stitching with the other. However, especially when working with a larger piece of canvas it helps to use a frame. Without a frame the canvas can be badly pulled out of shape, particularly if you tend a stitch too tightly. Working with a frame also leaves both hands free so that one hand may be used above and the other one below the canvas, allowing the needle to pass back and forth from front to back, and allowing you to stitch faster. Stitches worked on a frame are more even than those made when a canvas is hand held. There are several types of frame to choose from and my advice would be to visit your local needlework shop where they will advise you on which type of frame, if any, is most suitable for you. Each person should work in the way that they feel most comfortable with, whether it is to work with a frame or to hold the work in the hand. I personally like to stitch my design hand-held not only because my tension is even and not too tight therefore requiring little stretching afterwards, but more importantly, so that I can carry it around with me-stitching in the garden, on the train, visiting friends.

To prepare the Canvas

If you wish to duplicate the exact size of my needlepoint designs as given in this book, use the size of canvas as given with the instructions for each design. The measurements include a margin of extra canvas all around the needlepoint design. This margin varies from approx 1" (3.75cm) for small pieces (picture frames, spectacle cases etc.) to 3" (7.5cm) for the larg-

est pieces. This excess is later trimmed when the backing is sewn on.

Before you start to stitch, you need to mark onto the canvas the outside dimensions of the needlepoint design. Fold the canvas in half in both directions to find the centre. With a waterproof pen (never use a pencil as it rubs off onto your work) or coloured thread, mark the centre lines, vertically and horizontally. This divides the design into quarters which makes it easier to count.

Now count the canvas threads, one for each chart square, to determine the size of the charted design area (the number of stitches for height and width for each piece is given with the instructions for each needlepoint design). Mark the outside dimensions.

If you decide to use a frame, now is the time to assemble the canvas on to it. If the needlepoint is to be hand held, it helps to over-stitch or tape the edges of the canvas to prevent them fraying or catching.

Needlepoint Stitches

There are many types of stitches used for needlepoint but for the purpose of the designs in this book, where the emphasis is on colour and bold pattern, rather than on textural interest and stitch contrast, only one basic type of stitch is used. This is known as the tent stitch. This stitch can be worked in a number of different ways - the half-cross stitch technique, the continental technique and the basket weave technique. All three techniques are quick and easy and from the front of the work create the same short, slanting stitches. It is at the back of the canvas that they differ. Each technique has its advantages and disadvantages. If you are a beginner try all three and use which ever you are most comfortable with. You can use different

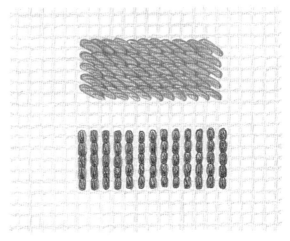

Back of the canvas showing the differences between tent stitch worked, using the continental techniques (above) and using the half-cross technique (below)

techniques on the same canvas but for larger areas stitched in one colour, it is best to keep to one technique to avoid forming ridges on the right side of the work.

Half-Cross Techniques

Of the three techniques used for working tent stitch,

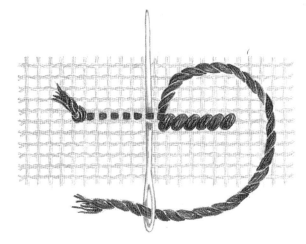

To start tent stitch using the half-cross technique. Work the first row of stitches from right to left as shown, making short vertical stitches at the back. To start work over the loose end at the back of canvas see page 149

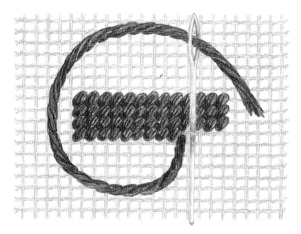

Work the following rows of stitches below the last row, stitching alternately from right to left and then left to right. The needle will point alternately upwards and downwards with each row.

the half-cross technique, is the easiest and uses the least amount of yarn. It forms shorter vertical stitches on the back, which do not completely cover the back of the canvas, thus creating a thinner needlepoint than one worked using the other two tent-stitch techniques. If you choose to use this technique over a

large area of solid colour, ideally it should be worked on a canvas held taut in a frame. This is because all the stitches in the piece pull in one direction from left to right, and the canvas can become very distorted. I like to use this method for filling in small areas. This technique should be worked on an interlock or double-thread canvas.

Continental Technique

This technique forms longer, slanting stitches on the back, which completely cover the back of the canvas,

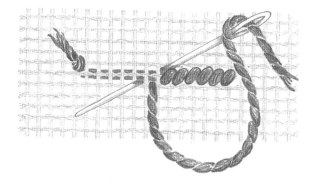

To start tent stitch using the continental technique. Work the first row of stitches from right to left a shown, making long slanting stitches at the back of the canvas. Work over loose end at the back as described below.

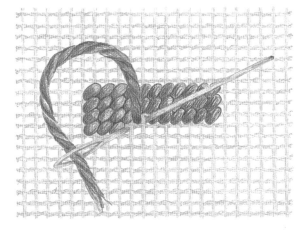

Work the following row of stitches below the last row, stitching alternately from right to left, and then left to right. If the work is hand held you can turn the canvas upside down after each row so you will always work from right to left.

resulting in a thicker, firmer needlepoint than one worked in half-cross technique. This makes it very suitable for designs to be used for upholstery (e.g.

footstools, chair seats etc.) This technique can be worked on any type of canvas.

Basketweave Technique

This is an excellent technique for covering large areas of background. Unlike the half-cross and continental techniques it is worked in diagonal rows. At the back of the work, the stitches change direction with each row, pulling the canvas both ways alternately so very little, if any distortion of the canvas occurs. This technique can be worked on any type of canvas.

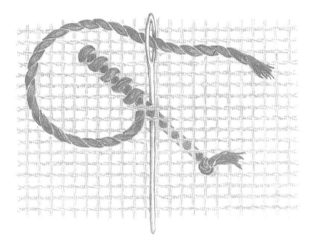

To start tent stich using the basketweave technique. Work the first row of stitches downwards diagonally from left to right, making vertical stitches at the back of the canvas. Work over the loose end at the back as described below.

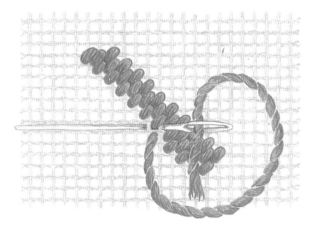

Work the following row of stitches upwards, from right to left, slotting in between the stitches of the previous row and making horizontal stitches at the back of canvas work

To Start and Finish Stitching

I can not stress enough how important it is when stitching not to use too long a length of yarn. The length should be no longer than 20" (50cm). Longer lengths are more difficult to work, tending to twist and knot. Additionally, the yarn can wear thin in which case it may no longer cover the canvas adequately.

Although tent stitch can be worked in a number of ways (see above) the method of starting and finishing the ends of the yarn is the same for each technique. Care should be taken to start and finish off each strand of wool properly. To start: knot one end of the yarn. Insert your needle through the canvas about 1" (2.5cm) from where you intend to start, leaving the knot on the right side. As you work, your stitches will hold the yarn in place at the back and the knot can be sniped off when it is reached. To finish off: take the remaining length of yarn to the back of the work and thread through at least six stitches before cutting off.

Tension

When stitching it is important to have an even tension. The term tension means how tightly each stitch is pulled. If your tension is too tight, the canvas may become puckered and the finished needlepoint will be slightly smaller in size. The wool will be stretched and become thin and uneven. If your tension is too loose, loops will form and it will not be neat. Try to keep the tension of each stitch even throughout and the resulting work will be smoother. This will all come with a little practice and is easier if working on a frame.

Unpicking Stitches

If an area of stitching needs to be undone, due to a mistake, great care must be taken not to damage the canvas. I find it easier to carefully snip each stitch with a pair of small pointed scissors and then to pull out the cut ends using tweezers.

If during unpicking, you do cut a canvas thread by mistake, do not panic, it is easy to repair. Cut a small piece of blank canvas from the side of your work and place behind the damaged area, aligning the position of the holes, and the threads. Work the new stitches through both the original canvas and the patch.

Working from a Chart

All my needlepoints come in chart form and contrary to what many people think, working from a chart is very simple. It just requires careful counting. Each square on the chart represents one stitch. As each stitch is worked over a thread of canvas, you count the threads rather than the holes of the canvas. Each square is coloured in a shade as near as possible to the original wool colour. Sometimes, however, the colours are very similar and to make each one distinguishable from the other the colouring on the chart

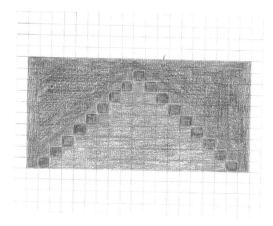

Detail of a chart.

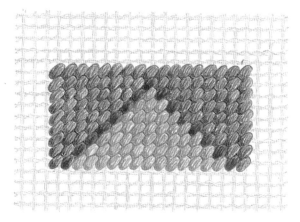

Detail of a worked canvas showing lines created by the slant of the stitches.

will be exaggerated for clarity. The colour key provides the exact colour to be used and you should also refer to the photograph.

Where you start to stitch is, I think, a matter of preference. Ideally work the design first and then fill in the background afterwards. I like to start each design from the centre and to work outwards. If you prefer to start from an outside edge, start from the upper right or left-hand corner and work diagonally downwards so that you are not repeatedly rubbing over areas already stitched. Make sure that the top of the needlepoint corresponds to the top of the chart. If a design is worked in the wrong direction the shapes will alter, because of the slant of the stitch. In this book the top of the chart is always at the top of the page. If you find it difficult reading the charts in this book, or you do not wish to continually carry the book around with you, may I suggest that you colour photocopy the chart. I always do this and then I can scribble notes onto the copy. If the chart is split across two or even four pages, each section of chart can be taped together. If you find the squares of each chart too small to read easily, have a colour enlargement copy made.

Finishing the Needlepoint: Stretching

Before a completed needlepoint can be made up it may require stretching first, especially if it has become distorted during stitching and has not been worked on a frame. Do not trim the canvas until stretching has been completed.

To stretch a needlepoint you will need a clean board which must be larger than the canvas and soft enough to take tacks easily, a large set-square, a hammer, and carpet tacks or drawing pins.

Place the finished needlepoint face down and dampen it thoroughly by spraying it with water, or using a damp sponge. Be careful not to soak the needlepoint. Then stretch the needlepoint into shape (don't be afraid to be quite firm) and nail all around the edge of the canvas, continually tugging into

Dampen the back of the work thoroughly before stretching.

Stretch needlepoint, securing into shape with either carpet tacks or drawing pins.

shape. Either begin with a nail at the centre of each side and then work outwards to the corner, or the method which I prefer is to nail one entire side before going onto the next. For both methods it is a good idea to use a set square to check that each corner is at a right angle.

If the canvas is badly distorted steam on the wrong side with either a kettle or a steam iron, being careful not to touch the needlepoint with the iron. Allow the needlepoint to dry completely before removing the tacks even if it takes several days. If the piece is still distorted, repeat the process.

To Join two Pieces of Needlepoint

The best method for joining two pieces of needlepoint along a straight fold line is to use tent stitch, worked using the half-cross technique. After stretching the finished needlepoint, trim the canvas edge to $\frac{1}{2}$" (1cm) and fold back the canvas along the seam line. This fold should follow the next line of the canvas thread,

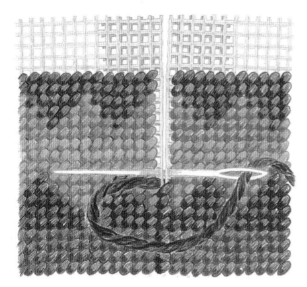

Joining two pieces of needlepoint.

and not fall across the canvas holes. With the right sides of the needlepoint facing, line up the edges row by row. Using the colour of yarn as specified in the needlepoint instructions, fasten at the back of the canvas and bring the needle through to the front, passing through the first hole at the lower edge of the right-hand piece. Now take the needle through the second hole of the adjacent piece to the wrong side and then back through to the front again, passing this time through the second hole on the right hand piece. Continue in this way up the seam, making half-cross stitches. When the seam is complete, fasten off at back of work.

Backing a Cushion

Most designs in this book are for cushions. Backing a cushion is a simple process and if you don't have a machine, hand stitching is equally suitable. The material you choose should be reasonably thick, particularly if it is to be a floor cushion. I prefer to use a medium weight Indian cotton, easily available in a wonderful assortment of strong colours. Fine wools and upholstery velvet are also suitable. Take care when choosing the colour of your backing material. It should enhance, not distract from the design. If in doubt, choose a colour that matches the background colour of your needlepoint. Zips are optional, but they do allow the cushion pad to be removed easily. Alternatively you can leave a gap at the bottom of a cushion, stitching it up after the cushion pad has been inserted.

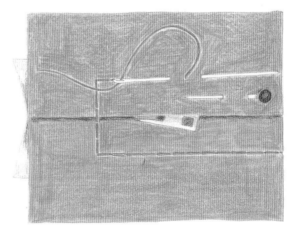

Inserting a zip fastener.

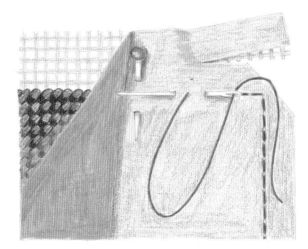

Stitch the backing fabric to the needlepoint using small backstitches or a sewing machine.

If inserting a zip fastener, you will need to cut two pieces of fabric. To calculate the size, divide the area of the stretched needlepoint in half widthways and add to each piece 5/8" (1.5cm) seam allowance all round. With right sides facing, join at each end of the centre seam, leaving enough seam open in the middle for the length of the zip fastener. Pin and tack the zip fastener into position and stitch, using a sewing machine with a zip foot or by hand using backstitch.

If you are not using a zip fastener, you will need to cut one piece of fabric, the area of the needlepoint plus $\frac{5}{8}$" (1.5cm) seam allowance all round.

With right sides facing (the zip open, if you are using one) pin and tack the needlepoint to the backing. If using cord or piping, read the section on 'Edgings' before going any further. Stitch as close as possible to the needlepoint edge using small stitches. Remember, if no zip fastener is being used to leave a gap just big enough to insert a cushion. Trim excess canvas and clip the corners diagonally to minimize bulk. Turn cushion cover right side out and insert cushion pad.

Edgings, Cord and Piping

Both cord and piping, when sewn to the edge of a cushion, make a simple but effective finish.

Always remember when working with cord that it unravels very quickly if the ends are not bound with a small piece of sellotape after cutting. It is best to start along the bottom edge of the needlepoint either at the end of the gap left for inserting the cushion pad, or if a zip fastener is used, at a $\frac{1}{2}$" (1cm) gap left in the seam when stitching backing to needlepoint. With the cushion cover right side out, push 1" (2.5cm) of cord into the gap and sew into position, using double cotton or button thread and a curved needle. Sew cord along right side of seam edge, round back to starting point. As you sew, be careful not to pull the cord tight. It should lie easily. Push the second end of the

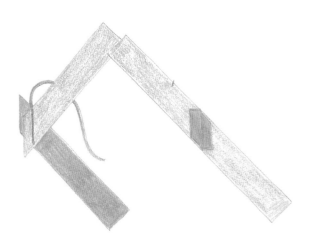

Join binding strips. Trim the seam corners.

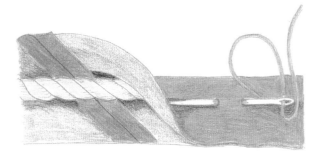

Stitch binding close to cord.

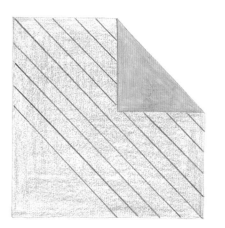

Mark out strips along the bias of the piping fabric and cut.

Pin piping between backing fabric and needlepoint and stitch together using small backstitches or a sewing machine.

cord in next to the first end and stitch this and the gap firmly together.

Piping is made from fabric cut on the bias and wrapped around piping cord. The fabric used can either be the same as the backing fabric or a contrasting fabric. Piping cord is available in a range of thickness, so you can decide how prominent you want it. Cut biased fabric into strips wide enough to wrap round the cord and to allow $\frac{1}{2}$" (1cm) on each edge for seam allowances. Join the strips by working a seam along the grain of the fabric. Press the seams. Wrap the binding round the cord, wrong sides facing and stitch as close to the cord as possible. Place the cord to the right side of the needlepoint piece, matching the stitching line of the covered piping to the edge of the needlepoint. Place the backing fabric over the piping and pin all three together. To join ends, first join the binding strips with a flat seam along the grain of the fabric. Unravel the two sides of piping cord and trim strands at different lengths. Overlap ends by 1" (2.5cm). Intertwine to make a smooth join. Stitch in place and trim as for Backing Cushion, above.

Cleaning Needlepoint

Needlepoint when dirty can either be washed with warm water and a gentle soap powder or dry cleaned. I think it is better to have your needlepoint pieces dry cleaned, especially if they have been made up into cushions. Always check before starting whether the yarns you have used have any special washing or dry cleaning instructions and also check your backing fabric to make sure it is colourfast. I use the bath when washing my work so I can lie it flat, right side down. Always be very gentle, never squeeze or rub your needlepoint. Use a large sponge to press up and down on the back, to ease the dirt out. When rinsing change the water frequently. After the final rinse, let the bath or sink empty and use a clean, dry sponge to soak up as much excess water as possible. Lie the needlepoint onto a large thick towel and very gently roll it up. This will help to get rid of any further excess water. Finally re-stretch the piece (see page 150).

If a piece of needlepoint has been used to cover a piece of furniture, washing in the bath or dry cleaning is impossible. Vacuum clean thoroughly to remove as much dirt as possible and then sponge with an upholstery detergent, reading the instructions carefully first.

Picture Frame

All you need for completing each of your needlepoint frames, is stiff cardboard and strong masking tape. On a piece of paper, measure and draw the dimensions of your finished and stretched needlepoint. When you measure, ignore the 2 outer rows of stitches all round the edge of the needlepoint. This is to allow the outer row of stitches to overlap the card to the inside (when assembling the frame, if this is still not possible trim the cardboard to the required measurement). Trace the outline of the frame twice onto a piece of cardboard. Cut the shapes, the first with a hole in the centre for the front of the frame and the second shape without a hole. Trim the excess canvas, leaving a 1" (2.5cm) edge all round. Cut the outer corners diagonally and slit the inner corners as shown in the illustration. Carefully position the cardboard piece for the front of the frame over the back of the needlepoint. Fold only one outer side edge of the canvas over the frame and tape securely in place, making sure the needlepoint is straight. I find using clothes pegs or bulldog clips excellent for this job. All overlap can be correctly positioned and held in place before finally taping or gluing. Leave the three remaining outer edges free. Fold over all the inside edges and tape in place. Position the cardboard piece for the back of the frame over the back of the front piece. Fold the three remaining outer edges over the back of the frame and tape. Slide your picture into position through the open edge.

Position the cardboard piece for the front of the frame over the back of needlepoint.

Rug

Although I have not stitched a rug for this book, I have suggested with several of my designs (e.g. Lady's Bouquet page 25) that working 2, 4 or even 6 pieces in that particular design and then joining them together would make a glorious rug.

Making a rug is not difficult. The simplest and most manageable way is as mentioned above, to join together separate squares of needlepoint. A rug made from a single piece of canvas is often too heavy and awkward to stitch. It is important to remember when making a rug that each square of needlepoint must use the same mesh size and type of canvas. Each adjoining side must have the same number of stitches so that each square can be joined stitch for stitch. All stitches in a completed rug should run in the same direction.

The pieces of needlepoint are joined together by overlapping their canvas edges and then stitching through both layers. The threads and holes of the canvas must be lined up exactly. I usually allow three rows of stitching to join my rug squares. When the pieces are to be joined, leave the underneath one untrimmed. Trim the top canvas between the third and fourth thread (this does depend on seam width). Work three rows of stitches through both layers. Any little ends of canvas that stick up, just snip out. When four pieces of needlepoint join, you will have to stitch through four layers of canvas.

Depending on the designs used for a rug, I either join each piece using the same background colour or make a feature of the seam and use a contrasting colour to create a frame for each square. This also applies to the outside edge of the rug. After folding excess canvas all round the outside edge to wrong side, I stretch in either the same shade as the outermost row of my design or in a contrasting colour. For a good strong edge first stitch over the fold one way all round and then back again.

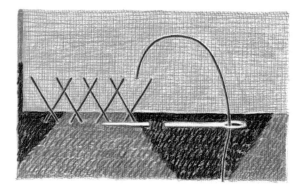

Herringbone stitch.

To line the rug I would recommend upholstery Hessian as a good backing fabric. First Herringbone stitch all loose edges of canvas to the wrong side of the rug so that it lies flat (see illustration). Cut the lining to the finished area of the rug plus 1" (2.5cm) seam allowance all around. To stop the lining bagging it should be attached to the back of the carpet with rows of stitches. This is done by working a small stitch through the lining and catching the back of the

rug. Bring the needle back up, running the thread under the lining to make the next stitch. I usually work a central line of stitching from top to bottom and then another line from side to side. For larger rugs, further rows of stitching may be required to prevent bagging. Turn under the seam allowances of the lining and slip stitch it to the rug edges.

Framing a needlepoint with fabric.
The Lord and Lady Washington design (page 98) is a good example of how fabric can be used to frame a finished needlepoint. I used a plain coloured cotton fabric but for a more complex effect you could use a patterned fabric, but make sure it doesn't dominate the design.

For the frame you will need to cut four strips of fabric. The length of each strip will measure the length of each side of the needlepoint (thus if the design is square all pieces will be the same length) and the width will measure the width of the border. This depends on how big you want the frame. I chose a 2" (5cm) width. Cut the strips on the straight grain of the fabric and add ⅝" (1.5cm) all round for seam allowance. Join the strips diagonally at each corner, using a sewing machine, or by hand using backstitch. Do not stitch the seam allowance at the inside edge. Trim the seam and press open. With right sides facing pin and tack fabric frame along inside edge to outer edge of needlepoint. Stitch as close to the needlepoint as possible. Trim excess canvas. To back the framed needlepoint follow instructions for backing a cushion (page 151).

Bags
These instructions are for the completion of the Cossack Jewel designs on Pages 134-43. All measurements given in these instructions are those I used for my own needlepoint bags. Chose your own measurements depending on what size you want your bag.

Making a bag is a very simple process. Choose a reasonably thick fabric that complements your needlepoint, just as you would if you were backing a cushion. I wanted my bags to be luxurious so I chose velvet.

For Cossack Jewel designs 1, 2 and 4 work as follows (referring to the photographs): For each bag you will need to cut two pieces of fabric. For the back of the bag cut one piece the area of the needlepoint plus an extra 6" (15cm) in length. For the top front border cut a piece the width of the needlepoint and 6" (15cm) in length. For each piece add ⅝" (1.5cm) all round for seam allowance. With right sides facing pin and tack the top front border to the top edge of the needlepoint. Stitch as close to the needlepoint as possible. Trim excess canvas. Then back bag just as you would a cushion but remember to leave the top open. Hem top edge of bag. Fold fabric above needlepoint in half to wrong side and secure into position with a few stitches on each side seam. Sew on cord along seam edges if required. Refer to Edgings (page 152)

For designs 3 and 5 the fabric frames the needlepoint at the front on three sides. Work as follows (referring to the photographs):

For the back and sides of the bag cut one piece the area of the needlepoint plus an extra 4" (10cm) in width and 6" (15cm) in length. For the top front border cut a piece the width of the needlepoint and 6" (15cm) in length. For each piece add ⅝" (1.5cm) all round for seam allowance. Join the top front border to the top edge of the needlepoint as above. Trim excess canvas. With right sides facing join side edges of backing to side edges of needlepoint. Trim excess canvas. Join lower edge making sure that the fabric borders on either side of the needlepoint are even in width. Complete bags as for those above.

Charting your own designs

The art of translating pattern onto canvas for needlepoint is not difficult, even less so if one limits oneself to a few basic stitches. I like to concentrate on the colour and pattern of a design rather than on texture created by the use of various technical skills. Here are some hints to consider when creating your own designs. It is very important to get the scale of a design right and where you place the motifs, particularly pictorial ones. Remember the edges of a cushion or a chair cover are often obscured when completed. So don't put your best details where they can not be seen. I first decide on what I am going to make (eg cushion, chair cover, bag) and the size of the finished needlepoint. Then I choose the type and most importantly the gauge of the canvas I will be working with (see page 146). Whether a design is geometric or pictorial I always draw directly onto graph paper. Each square of graph paper represents one stitch. I draw the parameters of the design onto the paper and then work the design within this space. I frequently move the parameters a few stitches either way, particularly when I want to achieve a symmetrically arranged geometric pattern. Don't forget, improvise. When you choose your colours be careful not to pick colours that are too dark. Each stitch creates a little shadow, so choose a slightly lighter colour and it will be the right shade when stitched. Although I like to decide on all my colours before I start stitching I often find myself changing one or two of them. But remember be patient. You need to stitch quite a large are of pattern before you can see if all the colours are working together

Conversion Chart

Wherever possible the nearest available equivalent colour has been chosen.

DMC	Appleton	Anchor	Paterna	DMC	Appleton	Anchor	Paterna
7107	502	8218	970	7465	302	9490	435
7108	503	8218	840	7473	873	8022	733
7110	505	8220	940	7491	984	9362	455
7125	864	8234	853	7492	691	9322	444
7127	504	8204	840				
7146	206	8308	872	7501	691	9322	444
7147	147	8352	910	7506	695	8100	732
7167	714	9600	480	7512	902	7513	9406
7168	207	8312	870	7533	587	9648	420
7169	126	9600	481	7535	588	9666	459
7196	225	8400	D211	7541	645	9078	D516
7198	226	8402	D211	7542	831	9004	D522
				7548	253	9164	693
7202	754	8412	914	7583	253	9196	693
7205	145	8420	912	7593	322	8736	513
7209	758	8422	900				
7226	714	8508	921	7650	566	8822	502
7241	101	8586	333	7690	155	8880	533
7251	602	8482	914	7692	152	8896	534
7273	964	9776	202	7702	155	8880	533
7297	748	8794	500	7709	102	8588	312
7299	852	8744	570	7724	761	9324	444
				7725	474	8060	725
7301	562	8814	503	7742	554	8120	711
7302	563	8818	504	7758	225	8400	931
7303	726	8312	860	7759	755	8400	D234
7304	564	8820	502				
7306	853	8792	501	7767	475	8100	723
7307	749	8636	571	7770	543	9166	693
7311	568	8794	500	7772	542	9094	694
7314	463	8644	551	7781	696	8102	731
7316	821	8630	542	7782	695	8024	732
7320	404	9006	611	7797	464	8690	542
7326	155	8900	533	7798	743	7798	562
7329	158	8884	531	7799	462	8686	544
7337	156	8882	532				
7356	721	8310	872	7828	563	8802	585
7361	241	9306	653	7840	932	9622	D123
7362	243	9216	652	7861	525	8936	522
7363	242	9218	651				
7364	243	9200	652	7909	832	8972	662
7376	355	9176	602	7911	427	8988	683
7377	356	9178	600	7920	866	8238	851
7398	296	9082	660	7926	565	8820	503
				7927	926	8898	522
7421	903	9406	441	7950	203	9616	874
7426	344	9260	602	7999	159	8906	530
7428	646	9026	D516	7996	463	8808	583
7432	185	9622	471				
7444	476	8062	722	ECRU	882	0386	263
7446	722	8310	871	NOIR	998	9800	221
7460	702	9632	475				

Lengths of different manufacturers skeins and hanks.

	SKEIN	HANK
DMC	8.8yd (8m)	
Appleton	10yd (9.2m)	60yd (55m)
Anchor	10.8yd (10m)	
Paterna	8yd (7.3m)	40yd (37m)

All of the alternative yarns are tapestry wool except for Paterna which is a stranded Persian yarn consisting of 3 strands. If you choose to use Paterna on a 10-mesh canvas and working in tent stitch, use all three strands of the yarn. For a finer 12 or 13-mesh canvas use only 2 strands of Paterna.

List of Suppliers

Canvas
If you have problems obtaining canvas contact DMC at the address below.

Needlepoint yarns
DMC tapestry wool has been used for all the designs in this book. If you wish to use Appleton, Anchor or Paterna wool as an alternative, see Conversion Chart on page 156. All these tapestry yarns are widely available in department stores and needlework shops. If you have problems finding a stockist near you, contact the yarn companies and main distributors as listed below:

DMC
UK: DMC CREATIVE
WORLD LTD,
Pullman Road,
Wigston,
Leicester.
LE8 2DY
England
Tel: 0533 811040

U.S.A: DMC
CORPORATION,
10 Port Kearny,
South Kearny,
New Jersey 07032.
Tel: 201 589 0606.

AUSTRALIA: DMC
NEEDLECRAFT PTY LTD,
51-56 Carrington Road,
Marrickville,
NSW 2204.
Tel: 2 559 3088

APPLETON
UK: APPLETON BROS LTD,
Thames Works,
Church Street,
Chiswick,
London
W4 2PE
England.
Tel: 081 994 0711

U.S.A: POTPOURRI ETC,
PO Box 78,
Redondo Beach,
California 90277

AUSTRALIA: CLIFTON H
JOSEPH & SON PTY LTD,
391-393 Little Lonsdale
Street,
Melbourne,
Victoria 3000

ANCHOR
U.K: COATS PATONS
CRAFTS,
McMullen Road,
Darlington,
County Durham,
DL1 1YQ
England
Tel: 0325 381010

U.S.A: COATS AND
CLARKS,
Susan Bates Inc,
30 Patewood Drive,
Greenville,
South Carolina 29615.
Tel: 1 800 648 1479

AUSTRALIA: COATS
PATONS CRAFTS,
89-91 Peters Avenue,
Mulgrave,
Victoria 3170.
Tel: 0325 381010

PATERNA
U.K: PATERNA LTD,
PO Box 1,
Ossett,
West Yorkshire
WF5 9SA
England
Tel: 0924 276744

U.S.A: JCA Inc,
35 Scales Lane,
Townsend,
Massachusetts 01469.
Tel: 508 597 8794

AUSTRALIA: ALTAMIRA,
34 Murphy Street,
South Yarra,
Melbourne,
Victoria 3141.
Tel: 3 867 1240

Kits

A selection of Mary Norden's needlepoint designs are available as kits from Ehrman. To order contact one of the following addresses:

U.K: EHRMAN.
14-16 Lancer Square,
Kensington Church Street,
London W8 4EP
England.
Tel: 071 937 8123

U.S.A: EHRMAN,
5 Northern Boulevard,
Amherst,
New Hampshire 03031.
Tel: 800 433 7899

AUSTRALIA: TAPESTRY
ROSE,
P.O. Box 366
Canterbury 3126
Victoria
Tel: 3 818 6022

If you wish to have a piece of furniture upholstered with needlepoint I can recommend no safer hands than those of David Scotcher

CONTACT: DAVID
SCOTCHER UPHOLSTERY,
285 Upper Street,
Islington,
London N1 2TZ
Tel: 071 354 4111

If you wish to buy a completed piece of needlepoint as illustrated in this book or you would like to commission a design please contact the author,
Mary Norden
c/o Weidenfeld & Nicolson Ltd.
Orion House, 5 Upper St Martin's Lane , London WC2 9EA

Acknowledgements

This book would never have been possible without the help and commitment from such a wonderful team of people. A very big thank you to the following: Joan Eve, June Harding, Phyllis and Rachael Kingman, Anne Newman, Mary Steening, Ann Steer and Pat Taylor for the many hours of stitching and working to such tight deadlines. Also David Scotcher who upholstered so beautifully the chair on page 127. I am also indebted to Malcolm Couch for his meticulous charts so calmly undertaken, Sarah Davies for her beautifully precise technical illustrations, and Frances Kelly, my agent, for her advice and encouragement. In addition, Omi and Mike Luckin, Gill and Roger Davies and Puff Fairclough who were wonderfully helpful and generous in allowing us to invade and disrupt their homes for photography, and Pip Rau for her kindness in lending many objects and reference books. I would also like to extend a special thanks to Hugh Ehrman for his help and enthusiasm.

In particular I am indebted to Nadia Mackenzie, who with great patience produced such glorious photographs, Roger Davies, who once again designed such a wonderful looking book and remained throughout so calm and diplomatic, and Yvette Cowles, who so delightfully handled publicity.

I am deeply grateful to Suzannah Gough, my editor, who brilliantly organized and guided the whole affair from its initial idea through to its colourful completion.

And lastly, a very special thank you to Charles for his continual support and for sharing my many hours of creative doubt and worry.

This book is dedicated to my parents.

Index